"Amazing Pets and Animals"

Inspired Poetry Animal Stories

Christina R Jussaume

2007 by Christina R Jussaume.
All rights reserved. No part of this book may be reproduced, stored in retrieval system or transmitted in any form by any means without the prior permission of the publishers, except by a reviewer who may quote brief passages in a review to be printed in a newspaper, magazine or journal.

ISBN 978-0-6151-8028-1

Dedication

My Husband, Daughter and Grandchildren

Author Acknowledgments

This collection is both enjoyable by children and adults. The Kitty Tales and Doggy Tales are actual pet story poems. There are some fables I have written and also some poems that have educational value about various species of animals. I also offer some short series poems that will take you to a fantasy land where you may see a flying dragon or a unicorn.
This collection is to be enjoyed by those that love animals.
I have also included five new poetry forms as tributes to people in my life that have made a significant difference to me.
My first book was **"My Walk with Jesus"** by PublishAmerica.

I would like to thank all the poets that have helped me achieve my dream of becoming a published author.
They have read my poetry on the poetry sites I belong to. They have helped me develop my talent and creativity.

**Special thanks to Poet
Patricia Ann Farnsworth-Simpson
For helping me with all the pictures
and cover design...**

&*****&

Newly Created Poetry Forms
By
Christina R Jussaume

Love for Eternity
(Joseph & Christina)

Now
You are both
In Heaven's gardens
I know you are both at peace
I know you appreciate
Serenity felt
By you both
There

&****&

Know that I do feel
Your lips like a seal
Feeling helps me deal

&****&

I cherish all memories that we shared
You both always cared when I was so scared
Any harm both sheltered from me and spared

&****&

I now know all this
We did share much bliss
This I now do miss

&****&

Await for me there
My poems I'll share
I'll make all aware

&****&

Poetry is key
Sharing I love thee
Poet I now be

&****&

In Memory of My Dad (Joseph's Star)

Dad
I miss you
I feel your presence
I sense you watch from above
I always looked up to you
When I see a star
I think of
You

&****&

Now
We're apart
I grieve no more now
My writing has helped me heal
I feel your spirit with me
Seventeen years now
You have been
Gone

&****&

Dad
I send love
Feel the breeze
When it blows, I send a kiss
Father remember this well
You were protector
On our dear
Earth

&****&

You
Still protect
I feel you in dreams
You are a part of my soul
You were my comforter too
I treasure our love
You're unique
Dad
&****&

Trusting Intuition
(Lucky Leaf)

Luck is just,
What you trust
Trust is believing in our dear Lord
The path with the light is one we trod
Believe in Master and you are on the right path
Forgive those that hurt you and try to hold down wrath
Believe in yourself too
Destiny will be true
Trust your heart
Forever

&*****&

Let spirit
Lead the way
Always listen to innermost thoughts
They guide and show us how to proceed
The spirit guides us on the path of the righteous
Always yield to the spirit's will throughout your life
Listen very closely
Follow advice given
It will be
Rewarding

&*****&

My Children (Michelle's Heart)

My children,
You're my prize.
I hope you are wise.
You are growing so very fast.
You are being taught things that will last.
It's important that you do understand.
Listen and learn all that you can.
Work hard and life will be great.
Always do respect,
Love of God
Forever

&*****&

I love you,
More each day.
Stay safe, this I pray.
Be honest in what you may do.
Honor values and always be true.
Be proud of what you may do in your life.
Pray to God for relief from strife.
Be good example for all.
Take care of yourself,
Always eat
Healthily.

&****&

Message of Hope and Peace
(Patricia's Harmony)

Peace I send to all
Attempt to help all achieve
Try to give all hope

&*****&

Reflecting on God
In words I may write each day
Comfort all oppressed

&****&

In uplifting verse
Assuring of God's value
Supporting Heaven

&****&

Hear angel's singing
Among Archangel Michael
Reassuring me

&****&

Make plans becoming worthy sheep
On occasion efforts you'll reap
Never doubt power of our Lord
Yes turn from bad, path of light trod

&****&

Table of Contents Page 1

Teaching Children about Pets	Page 14
The Pheasant	Page 16
Kitty Tales Part 1	Page 17
Kitty Tales Part 2	Page 19
The Rooster and the Hen (Fable)	Page 20
The Farmer (Fable)	Page 21
Kitty Tales Part 3	Page 22
Kitty Tales Part 4	Page 24
The Austrian Kookaburra	Page 26
Farmer John and the Barn Owl	Page 28
Kitty Tales Part 5	Page 29
Kitty tales Part 6	Page 30
Mary Jane and the Sheep (Fable)	Page 32
The Peacock and the Fox (Fable)	Page 33
Kitty Tales Part 7	Page 34
Kitty Tales Part 8	Page 35
Charles New Pet	Page 36
Dolphins at Play	Page 38
Kitty Tales Part 9	Page 39
Kitty Tales Part 10	Page 40
The Dove's Courtship	Page 42
The Dance of the Butterflies and Bees	Page 44
Kitty Tales Part 11	Page 46
Kitty Tales Part 12	Page 48
Thumbelina, the Smallest Horse	Page 50
A Horse's Golden Years	Page 51
The Fashion Show (Fable)	Page 53
The New Neighbor (Fable	Page 54
Kitty Tales Part 13	Page 55
Kitty Tales Part 14	Page 56
The Greyhounds (Fable)	Page 57
The Homeless Kitten	Page 58
The Llama	Page 60
Kitty Tales Part 15	Page 61
Kitty Tales Part 16	Page 62
I'm Randy the Robin	Page 64
The Cardinal	Page 65
Kitty Tales Part 17	Page 66
Kitty Tales Part 18	Page 67

Table of Contents Page 2

The Animal's Talent Show (Quatrain)	Page 69
Kitty Tales Part 19	Page 71
Kitty Tales Part 20	Page 72
Kitty Tales Part 21	Page 73
The Animal Talent Show Part 2 (Quatrain)	Page 74
Kitty Tales Part 22	Page 76
The Animal's Jamboree Part 3 (Quatrain)	Page 77
Kitty Tales Part 23	Page 78
Kitty Tales Part 24	Page 79
A Bird's Flight (Quatrain)	Page 80
I'm Sam the Squirrel (Quatrain)	Page 81
The Stray Cat (Quatrain)	Page 82
Kitty Tales Part 25	Page 84
Kitty Tales Part 26	Page 85
Kitty Tales Part 27	Page 86
Kitty Tales Part 28	Page 87
The Wood Ducks (Quatrain)	Page 88
The Magical Kingdom	Page 89
Kitty Tales Part 29	Page 90
Kitty Tales Part 30	Page 91
The Sheep Family (Fable)	Page 92
The Raccoon's Dilemma	Page 94
The Turtle and the Hare (Fable)	Page 95
Kitty Tales Part 31	Page 96
Kitty Tales Part 32	Page 97
The Squirrel Family (Quatrain)	Page 98
Life of a Bear (Quatrain)	Page 99
The Giraffe Family (Fable)	Page 100
Kitty Tales Part 33	Page 101
Kitty Tales Part 34	Page 102
Kitty Tales Part 35	Page 103
The Unicorn Family (Quatrain)	Page 104
The Dragon Family (Quatrain)	Page 106
The Donkey's Story (Quatrain)	Page 108
Kitty Tales Part 36	Page 110
A Calico Named Patches	Page 111
Kitty Tales Part 37	page 112
Kitty Tales Part 38	Page 113
Kitty Tales Part 39	Page 114

Table of Contents Page 3

Tinniesville (Quatrain)	Page 116
Tinniesville Part 2 (Quatrain)	Page 118
Tinniesville Part 3 (Quatrain)	Page 119
Kitty Tales Part 40	Page 120
Kitty Tales Part 41	Page 122
The Raccoon	Page 123
The Hawk (Tanka)	Page 124
The Eagle (Nonet)	Page 125
Doggy Tales Part 1	Page 126
Doggy Tales Part 2	Page 128
Doggy Tales Part 3	Page 129
The First Easter Bunny (Quatrain)	Page 130
Peter's First Fundraiser (Quatrain)	Page 132
Peter's Fundraiser Results (Quatrai n)	Page 134
Doggy Tales part 4	Page 136
Doggy Tales Part 5	Page 137
The Zoo Arrivals (Quatrain)	Page 138
Zoo Job Assignments (Quatrain)	Page 140
Doggy Tales Part 6	Page 142
Heathersville (Quatrain)	Page 144
Heathersville's Comeback Part 2	Page 146
Heathersville Part 3 (Quatrain)	Page 147
Doggy Tales Part 7	Page 148
Doggy Tales Part 8	Page 150
Heathersville Part 4	Page 151
Heathersville Part 5	Page 152
The Tiger's Plight	Page 153
The Flying Squirrel	Page 154
Heathersville Part 6	Page 155
Heathersville Part 7	Page 156
The Bear Family (Fable)	Page 157
The Prairie Dog (Haiku/Senyru)	Page 158
The Sly Skunk (Haiku)	Page 160
The Miniature Donkeys (Quatrain)	Page 161
Glossary of Poetry Forms	Page 162
Glossary of Poetry Forms	Page 163
Glossary of Poetry Forms	Page 164
Glossary of Poetry Forms	Page 165

Teaching Children about Pets

All young children should know that pets require care.
You should give some responsibility for them to share.
They can help by putting their little food dishes down.
The pet's care should be done when they are around.

&****&

We got a kitten when my daughter was just about five.
She loved to play with it and their playtime did thrive.
I explained that I needed to keep the kitty box clean.
She watched me disinfect each week to be pristine.

&****&

I taught her never to abuse by pulling their short tail.
I taught her to love them even when mischief did prevail.
I showed her that all pets must be treated with respect.
She learned they had to go to the Vets to be checked.

&****&

She did learn that I would never hit a very bad kitten.
No one should ever harm or hurt an animal by smitten.
All animals were created by Jesus or us on earth to see.
They all were important even the tiniest bumble bee.

&****&

At young age she learned care was needed to keep well.
When kitty played a lot, their happiness she could tell.
When her kitten had a litter herself we did give some away.
A neighbor had lost a kitten and our gift made their day.

&****&

In this instance she was taught to share to someone in need.
She felt good giving the kitten and it had been a good deed.
Later I explained that her cat would not be having any more.
We kept the Mother cat and two kitten which we did adore.

&****&

The Pheasant

I headed outside with a container of corn.
A male pheasant strolled by in early dawn.
I was in shock, as was only five feet away.
This experience really did make my day.

&*****&

He knew exactly where the corn was, too.
He hid in bushes, as I knew he would do.
I left for work, but knew he would return.
He'd satisfy hunger with corn he did yearn.

&****&

I watched from doorway as squirrel hid stash.
This wildlife view was better than any cash.
He dug holes and then would plant his corn.
I'm glad he's under pines, and not on the lawn.

&****&

Now I say I've fed fox, skunk, deer and pheasant.
To watch them inside my home is always pleasant.
The skunk is one I would not want to get near.
Now seeing the fox does not bring me any fear.

&****&

I find joy feeding wildlife that God gave as a gift.
Watching them all stroll through does truly uplift.
God created many species to bring us joy.
I marvel at the beauty of fish known as Koi.

&****&

Kitty Tales Part 1

My first cats were Fluffy, Tamatha, and Mittens.
Here is their story bringing them up as kittens.
Fluffy was a soft grey and white angora cat.
She was a small petite cat, and in no way fat.

&****&

She went in heat before I realized her age.
If I had known I would have kept her in a cage.
A short time later she became a young mother.
She then bred Tamatha and Mittens her brother.

&****&

They were really mischievous as all kittens are.
They scattered each time they did hear sound of a car.
I came home and went into the bathroom and saw,
Shredded toilet paper which they had used to claw.

&****&

Not long after, staging was put up near the house.
Mittens climbed all the way up in chasing a mouse.
He meowed loud as he was afraid to come down.
I sent husband up to return Mittens to ground.

&*****&

Another day Tammy sat on the curtain rod.
My husband saw this, and he gave me knowing nod.
She climbed unto his shoulders and then she got down.
Having these kitties, pleasure was always around.

&****&

All of these kittens mentioned we did truly love.
They all were called to attend to matter above.
I believe they all play in heavens of our God.
They are happy in the presence of our dear Lord.

&****&

Kitten Tales Part 2

Fluffy was gold fluffy cat I started to feed.
He hung around and he appeared to be in need.
He was friendly male but his fur was clumpy mess.
I really started to love him, I must confess.

&****&

We took to Vet to check his health and get his shots.
His fur was mostly shaved to get rid of the clots.
He was neutered so that he would then stay around.
After all this was done, he became comical clown.

&****&

Husband cutting lawn came in to get some relief.
Fluffy took charge sitting on seat to our belief.
I can still picture him as he just laid all stretched out.
Fluffy was funniest kitten to have about.

&****&

A new cat followed Fluffy home to no avail.
This cat was a large fully grown black and white male.
Midnight went to the Vet also to be checked out.
He was neutered so he would not wander about.

&****&

These two males learned to play together each new day.
They were wonderful companions, what can I say.
Fluffy was in driveway when a friend came to call.
"He looks like my Sunshine although was not so tall.

&****&

I only live up the street, yet he prefers your home."
"Yes, and here he has a friend and is not alone."
These cats are joined with Fluffy, Tammy and Mittens.
In my dreams they all play merrily as kittens.

&****&

The Rooster and the Hen (Fable)

There was a rooster and a hen which live on the same farm.
Russell watched Henrietta, keeping always from harm.
He was sweet on her, as she gave him much love.
He always walked close to her, like a hand and glove.

&****&

Russell could be friendly to any of the hen.
He only had eyes for Henrietta, time and again.
All the other hens were jealous of her beau.
They pushed and shoved her, until Russell did know.

&****&

Russell would come around, and peck all in his way.
This was his way of showing he was having a bad day.
Henrietta would then run to meet him with pride.
All the other hen, then did all run and hide.

&****&

Soon the other hens felt it was better to be a friend.
As a friend, they would not have to worry about their end.
Russell became so happy to see Henrietta smile.
He had stopped all the jealousy for a little while.

&****&

The moral here, is not to let jealousy in your heart.
It cannot help a situation, just makes you further apart.
Let God's goodness help you, to act kindly to all you meet.
When living like this, all bad situations will be defeat.

&****&

The Farmer (Fable)

An old farmer had many animals on his farm.
He rose early to feed caring they came to no harm.
He had sheep, cow's, chickens and even a dog and cat.
He even had a pet hog that was actually quite fat.

&***&

He was a kind man, generous to all that were in need.
He did need help when he planted his garden from seed.
One day he noticed the hens hardly had laid any eggs.
He reached down into nests, getting a pain in his legs.

&****&

He would stay out in barn tonight to find out this cause.
He felt someone was stealing, breaking God's cherished laws.
A young lad came in taking eggs from one of the hen.
He would return again to probably steal again.

&****&

The farmer waited until he took it in his hand.
"Look here son, tell me why stealing is part of your plan?"
"I steal because all my family depends on me.
I am sorry sir, but we are hungry, please do see."

&****&

The farmer decides to give him a job helping him.
Now the boy is well fed and things are no longer dim.
The moral is not to steal, what does not belong to you.
That is being dishonest, and not a good thing to do.

&****&

Kitty Tales Part 3

Cocoa followed one of my cats and crept on stairs.
She was kitten needing love of human that cares.
We had to lure her and captured in a basket.
If we didn't, she would have ended up in casket.

&****&

She was tiny, totally black with large green eyes.
She loved to go outside and she became quite wise.
She was a great hunter and brought me many gifts.
Birds, rabbits and mice were among her many tiffs.

&****&

She would always come in each and every night.
I would call her and she ran in with great delight.
I loved her very much and she slept beside me.
She was precious and was all she could ever be.

&*****&

We went to shelter to purchase a new kitty.
We bought a nine month old male in the next city.
We called Jake and he was part of our family.
Jake liked to go outside and was very carefree.

&****&

Jake was beautiful grey and black tuxedo cat.
He was slender and was no way considered fat.
He loved us both jumping from one lap to other.
He considered me to be surrogate Mother.

&****&

Jake was quite unique in a certain sort of way.
I had to stop munchies as he would beg each day.
Among things he enjoyed were cheese curls and popcorn.
He was precious kitty loving us night and morn.

&****&

Both of these precious kitties have now left this earth.
Their arrival in heaven was their new rebirth.
They play with all my other kitties each new day.
I know they're all happy in their own special way.

&****&

Kitty Tales Part 4

This is about Joshua, my black and white cat.
He is the apple of my eye, I'll explain that.
He was from pet store given to me as surprise.
I was grieving for Jake, with tears in my brown eyes.

&****&

When I got home husband said, "Can you see what's new?"
On his shoulder was Josh and he said " He's for you."
Jake and Josh looked alike and were both tuxedoes.
Josh being nervous ran like flying torpedoes.

&****&

Josh loves to be petted as he sits on my lap.
Oftentimes he will cuddle there for quite a long nap.
He's high jumper and loved to play with mouse on pole.
He caught it on his leg and we could not console.

&****&

He made 4th of July memorable as well.
He had dislocated his front paw when he fell.
He wore a splint on his paw for six weeks or more.
The first time I saw him wearing it, I closed door.

&****&

Day before the fourth and splint was red, white and blue.
I did not expect him to look like flag so true.
When I carried him from the vets, they all did stare.
I was thankful that my cat has received great care.

&****&

Joshua my youngest now sleeps with me each night.
He knows how to cuddle up to me that's just right.
I hope you do enjoy the first story of Josh.
He is a precious kitty, sometimes at great cost.

&****&

The Australian Kookaburra

The legend says the stars and moon lighted the earth.
Spirits wanted all the creatures to have much mirth.
They wanted all happy with warmth of their bright light.
The light was very pleasant and brought great insight.

&****&

They needed someone special to awake them all.
Then one day they heard unique Kookaburra's call.
He had seen a small mouse from treetop and had caught.
He was hysterical laughing at prey he sought.

&****&

He was extremely loud and he sounded just great!
Spirits thought the trumpet sound would really awake.
They planned to talk to him in his home in gum tree.
They asked if he would like honor of awaking thee.

&****&

They are carnivorous eating crabs, bugs and birds.
They're large kingfisher and their call resembles words.
They will breed twice a year and nest in hollow tree.
They can easily become tame if fed by thee.

&***&*

The kookaburra asked, "What if I don't want to?"
"If answer is no, we will not send light to you.
All will live in darkness and would feel really blue."
"Ok, I'll take the job, it will be something new."

&****&

All must try to give the kookaburra respect.
If anyone laughed at him, all surely would regret.
Each day spirits lit fire and all day it did glow.
Kookaburra's laugh was something all here did know.

&****&

The kookaburra awoke all many a year.
All that heard his laughter felt he was really dear.
If you should visit Australia listen well.
The trumpeted laughter you hear you will then tell.

&****&

Farmer John and the Barn Owl

John found baby owl, raising for good use and a pet.
He cared for when helpless, and he did never regret.
He lived and worked in the largest barn of his farm.
He was precious, and would fly to land on his arm.

&****&

His Ma lost track of him and where he had gone.
John had found him lost, and looking very forlorn.
John named him Frank after a cousin he had lost.
Frank was swell and never was a bother or cost.

&****&

Frank enjoyed his work and kept barn rid of all pest.
In the daylight he slept high in hayloft in a fluffy nest.
If John went into barn; he then made noise of glee.
John would then talk to him, and then flew to thee.

&*****&

After he became a mature male; he left the farm more.
John prayed he find a mate and it would be as before.
On day John saw Frank come home with a lady owl.
John gave thanks, as he heard his hunting dogs howl.

&*****&

John named her Faith, and they were a match, divine.
Frank and Faith had little owls in a very short time.
All their family now resided on his country farm.
As endangered species; no one would ever do harm.

&****&

Kitty Tales Part 5

I was feeding my birds on a lovely spring day.
I felt something furry rub me in special way.
I looked down to see, skinny fully grown black cat.
He tried eating bird food, and I gave him a pat.

&****&

I began to feed him outside on porch each day.
I could not bring in, until I knew he would stay.
One night I turned on the porch light and skunk I seen.
A fluffy skunk was eating from his dish, maybe mean.

&****&

The next day this black cat went in to see our Vet.
He got his shots, got neutered and had no regret.
We named him Magic, as he loved to eat and run.
He is gorgeous now, and loves to run and have fun.

&****&

He gets along with Joshua and Cuddles too.
They just love the house; to him this is very new.
He has freedom to come, and go as he does please.
He has a lovely life of cat living with ease.

&****&

He is a great hunter, takes care of mice in yard.
He has great manner, and loving him is not hard.
He takes care of next door neighbor's yard very well.
He is an awesome cat; this is what I must tell.

&****&

Kitty Tales Part 6

It was mid winter, and expecting snow that night.
I heard a faint meow, and saw an awesome sight.
Tiny black kitten was crawling on the side stair.
I opened some cat food and prepared warm milk with care.

&****&

I watched as she ate over a can of cat food.
She then let me hold her, as she was in good mood.
She never asked to go outside, was content here.
She was very shy and seemed to have lots of fear.

&****&

She weighed only two pounds, and I got her to Vet.
He said Mother had rejected her, not to fret.
She had one cloudy eye that did not see quite well.
He felt she had felt trauma, and her life was hell.

&****&

She was given shots, spaded and returned to us.
Now she is lap kitty that returns love and trust.
She is totally black with these large greenish eyes.
Her name is Cuddles, and that name we felt quite wise.

&****&

Cuddles greets us when we come home from work at night.
She plays with Josh and Magic stopping them from fight.
She was little ball of fur that brought us great joy.
She keeps males in line as they just want to be boys.

&****&

Mary Jane and the Sheep (Fable)

Little Mary Jane was tending the farmer's sheep.
She was very tired, and actually fell asleep.
When she awoke; the sheep were nowhere to be found.
She looked and looked again, she looked all around.

&****&

She climbed up and down hill, and did not find a one.
She was sorry that she had slept; this was not fun.
She had to tell the farmer; he had no more sheep.
At that point; he felt Mary Jane he would not keep.

&*****&

She had been on job, and did not pay attention.
Her employer found out, he put on suspension.
The moral is always work hard; do not slack off.
The weather was damp; she now had a nasty cough.

&****&

It is best to try to be the best you can be.
If you try your hardest, success you will then see.
She had not paid attention and that was just wrong.
Now she does say, "My job did not last very long."

&****&

The Peacock and the Fox (Fable)

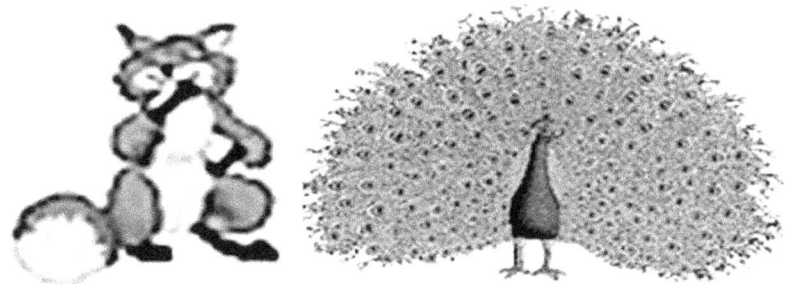

Patrick was prettiest peacock that all had seen.
He was kind of conceited, you know what I mean.
His owner would take pictures, to show to her friends.
Patrick never held a grudge, always made amends.

&****&

He often would get treats, faster that the others.
He was quite selfish, never sharing with brothers.
He did love a great big piece hunk of cheddar cheese.
As he ran to retrieve a piece; he then did sneeze.

&****&

A fox watched him, as he held unto the cheese tight.
She started to say that his beauty was great sight.
He listened to compliments, and then let cheese go.
She immediately snatched, as if she did know.

&*****&

Worshiping yourself is not what life is about.
Do not be conceited; of this I want to shout.
He lost his cheese, thinking that he was all glory.
This is the moral I have written in story.

&****&

Kitty Tales Part 7

One spring day, my cat Cocoa came home with male cat.
He was full grown, black with white paws needing some fat.
I fed him on stairs while she came in house to eat.
He lay on stairs later, getting out of the heat.

&****&

When I let her back out, they went off together.
They seemed to get along good in any weather.
He stayed for a while before we took to the Vet.
He checked out fine, was neutered and became great pet.

&****&

We called him Midnight, my teenage daughter's own cat.
With eating regular he gained a little fat.
He would sleep on her bed, each and every night.
He looked cute beside her as I turned out the light.

&****&

My belief was that Midnight was Cocoa's soul mate.
They were great for each other and it was their fate.
They were quite happy together for a few years.
Then he got sick and died and Cocoa shed her tears.

&*****&

I am thankful for time we did have with Midnight.
He gave us his love and trust and was a delight.
He is now with the other kitties with our Lord.
They all play together in the gardens of God.

&****&

Kitty Tales Part 8

It was weekday, and Hank left for work early morn.
It became noisy, and I heard a loud car horn.
I heard coyotes, and I saw with my own eyes.
Fluffy was under car, and I let out a sigh.

&****&

I ran down cellar and picked up a baseball bat.
I stood on the stairs screaming, and watching my cat.
They luckily were afraid and then left the yard.
I picked up Fluffy that was really shaking hard.

&****&

I had no fear as I must protect my young cat.
I was thankful that I did not face an attack.
Fluffy then went to sleep on my lap so content.
I was thankful I kept wits, and did not relent.

&****&

I had been Fluffy's own angel that day on earth.
Now he smiles down on a cloud above with much mirth.
I hope I always have the courage if need be.
Another time, I would call God to assist me.

&****&

Charles New Pet

Charles was a retired gent that lived in English town.
As widower, he kept busy without a frown.
He had a small cottage with a lovely garden.
His Border collie chased things out without pardon.

&****&

Molly was great friend and a great lovable dog.
They went for leisurely walks and sometimes would jog.
One day loud noise was heard as he was turning around.
He looked up and saw a beautiful owl made sound.

&****&

The owl was young and seemed to be trying to hunt.
They watched as he picked up a wee mouse very blunt.
Daily afterwards, they watched as he hunted food.
They then watched for him and both became in good mood.

&****&

Charles named Oliver and taught to perch on his arm.
Charles and Molly enjoyed his company and charm.
Charles built a basket that held Mollie on his bike.
The owl would fly ahead of them when on a hike.

&***&

The three of them went to tavern around midday.
The owl perched on bar counter in a real cute way.
They stayed a couple of hours while he drank a brew.
They would leave before dark as still were things to do.

&****&

The owl became quite a topic of attention.
Some wanted to borrow for rodent prevention.
Charles did not part with him no matter how they tried.
They were anxious to see and Charles often just sighed.

&****&

Dolphins at Play

"I'm Denny the dolphin, and here is my story.
My mate Donna often makes me feel much glory.
We are a star attraction at the Sea World Park.
I leap up high, as I am happy as a lark.

&****&

It is fun to be here, and have crowds come to see.
It makes Donna express her gratitude to me
We will be having a family very soon.
I believe it will be by the next full moon.

&****&

I know here we will always have plenty to eat.
Living here, there are no enemies to defeat.
We have our paradise here, just Donna and me.
With our family, our love will be bond to see.

&****&

On special occasion, some disabled swim inside.
Caretakers let them hold onto our fins so wide.
Their bodies are fluid in the water so blue.
They have so much joy on their faces that we view.

&****&

I feel happy we bring special humans great joy.
We are worth lots, and that's why they always employ.
How about it Donna, want to swim to our nook?
Alright you guys now it's time to go read a book."

&****&

Kitty Tales Part 9

It was spring day, and Magic was outside all day.
When I came home, he was on stairs laying strange way.
He had brown twig next to him which was very odd.
The things that cats may pick up on the path they trod!

&****&

He came in to eat, and then he went right back out.
I prepared supper and then I heard myself shout.
"Hank, do you want to go see our Grandkids tonight?"
"Sure, I think that will be a really great delight."

&****&

It was a great night to sit out on her large deck.
The children were playing together neck to neck.
Alexis was in awe at her little Brother.
He had been a gift from God to Dad and Mother.

&****&

We had great time and came home around nine that night.
In kitchen, it looked like there had been a bad fight.
All of our scatter rugs were all over the place!
Cuddles usually greets, and did not see her face.

&****&

Then I knew why, as a garden snake I did see.
The house cats had killed it, and then left to show me.
I screamed as then I knew the snake had been playing dead.
The twig was snake, and the cats had eaten his head!

&****&

Kitty Tales Part 10

My husband was cutting down some of our pine trees.
Magic was seen scratching from the bite from some fleas.
It became quite warm, and he took off his jacket.
The chainsaw was loud, and making quite a racket.

&****&

He accomplished quite a bit as I watched from inside.
Something ran into his side pocket to then hide.
He stacked all the wood in a really neat wood pile.
He felt tired, so he came in to rest for a while.

&****&

Joshua and Cuddles began to sniff his coat.
Then a grey mouse popped out and I cleared my throat.
I thought not much of it until cat pawed it hard.
The two cats started to chase it, mouse was in yard.

&****&

They cornered under the entertainment center.
This was our home but now I wished I was renter.
We both watched but the mouse was no way, coming out.
We went out to buy mouse traps and put them about.

&****&

A little while later we heard the mouse trap close.
He was scared and let out a smell nasty to nose.
The peanut butter made mouse extremely sticky.
My husband released outside as this was tricky.

&****&

I did not stay outside to see outcome of mouse.
I am just very thankful he's not at my house.

&****&

The Dove's Courtship

Two grey mourning doves met by the birdbath.
Female was splashing, getting rid of wrath.
Danny approached her hoping to get close.
He did splash around feeling hot as toast.

&****&

"My name is Denise," and she did splash back.
They then had fun in a playful attack.
"My name is Danny and you sure look fine.
Will you consider being mate of mine?"

&****&

Her answer was known when she cuddled near.
He nestled close to her finding her dear.
Together they then flew to grove below.
They sang to each other sweetly and slow.

&****&

Danny and Denise would be happy here.
The people here fed corn to birds and deer.
When on the ground, they would watch out for cat.
They saw one called Magic that was real fat.

&****&

Magic often watched them sitting on chair.
When he was on the porch, he did not care.
Magic was a black cat that they did love.
Often they said, "Stay away from those dove."

&****&

They felt that this place would make a nice home.
They were both happy they were not alone.
They had water, food and shade from the trees.
They even flew with butterflies and the bees.

&****&

The Dance of the Butterflies and Bees (Canzone)

The butterflies and the bees dance in motion.
It's like spell from love potion.
They know they are very much enjoyed by all.
Tending flowers is their call.

&****&

The sweet nectar is something they like to eat.
Watching them fly is real neat.
Both of them are very important creatures.
Butterfly has best features.

&****&

Both of these insects are needed for each bloom.
Without them, flowers have doom.
Everyone enjoys watching them fly all around.
They are airborne not on ground.

&****&

The butterfly only lives for a few days
Their courtship will just amaze.
They fly around another asking to mate.
Getting together is fate.

&****&

Later female lays her eggs on her host plant.
They start off real small, like ant.
Her life span is over before they are born.
They wake up in early morn.

&****&

Bees are needed for crops and for some honey.
Honey bees make you money.
Beekeepers learn to protect themselves from stings.
They enjoy money it brings.

&***&

The butterfly zoos attract many each year.
Viewing them is really dear.

Kitty Tales Part 11
The Magnificent Seven

My first seven cat's memories are a keepsake.
I had Fluffy, Mittens, Tamatha and a Jake.
There was a second Fluffy, Midnight and Cocoa.
Cocoa Mommy loved you the most, this you must know.

&****&

Cocoa even with your blindness, you still held on.
Sometimes I forget your not here and you are gone.
Joshua now sleeps with me as you did before.
My heart does ache for you, knowing you are no more.

&****&

Jake you were precious, even though you had a short time.
Whenever I do snack, I bring back a remind.
Cuddles does some of the things you always did do.
She will go from my lap to Dad's with a meow.

&****&

Tammy you are the only one not buried here.
You lived to be eighteen years of age and were dear.
My first Fluffy was white and grey and a kitten.
I adored as you gave me Tammy and Mittens.

&***&

Our second Fluffy was golden and quite a sap.
He many times lay on lawn mower for a nap.
Mittens you were a good mouser and earned your keep.
The night you got hit by a car, I lost much sleep.

&****&

Midnight you were an awesome lovable kitty.
You slept with Michelle each night looking so pretty.
You all are precious pieces kept within my heart.
I will always love you even though we're apart.

&****&

Play merrily in the gardens of our dear God.
I am happy knowing you are there with our Lord.
Until we do meet again be good kitty cats.
You are in my dreams that are a matter of fact.

&****&

Kitty Tales Part 12

My cat Joshua has a special bond with me.
He meowed loud until I opened eyes to see.
I had not been feeling well so I went to bed.
He sensed an asthma attack and awoke instead.

&****&

Fully awake now, I knew I needed machine.
The breathing treatment did give me great self esteem.
He ran right after me as I walked down the stairs.
He had returned his love showing me how he cares.

&****&

Josh does love to sit on my lap every night.
He gets upset if I spend too much time on site.
He and Cuddles are playmates while I am at work.
If I don't play with him, he sulks acting like jerk.

&****&

He might get attention by prancing around desk.
He then meows constantly to see who wins test.
Then he will begin to play with his scratching post.
Constant meowing does it, as I love him most.

&****&

I believe he is an angel sent from above.
He is very lovable, and I show my love.
He always senses whatever mood I am in.
He knows me like a book, as if he was my kin.

&****&

Thumbelina, the Smallest Horse

Thumbelina is the smallest horse in the world.
She visits children's hospitals with tail curled.
She is very short, just seventeen inches tall.
She will uplift all their spirits, this is her call.

&*****&

Her owners will not let her be a circus act.
She'll be in Guinness book of records, that's fact.
She is a fundraiser for the small children's care.
She has traveled many states so all are aware.

&****&

Most days she plays with farm dogs that are her size.
Her stable is a dog house as owners thought wise.
Her photo will be in the 2008 world book in the fall.
Her size has helped charities and this was her call.

&****&

She is loved by people and she loves attention.
She likes to be the attraction they do mention.
She has visited schools and summer camps too.
I know my feelings for her are warm and true.

&****&

The tinniest horse has a reason to survive.
She is the greatest fundraiser that's alive.
All that see her think she's just a precious sight.
She is loved by young and old and is a delight.

&***&

A Horse's Golden Years

A horse that was well loved was getting on in years.
His owner Mary often fought back her wet tears.
They had raised him from a colt and named him Sunday.
He had been born on Lord's Day, not on a Monday.

&****&

David and Mary both rode him on the prairie.
He had great personality and was merry.
Their Daughter Sue-Ellen found him gentle and kind.
He could be trusted with children and had sound mind.

&****&

He had a mate that was called Claire who stayed real near.
He became blind and with her close he had no fear.
They were fenced in a large field they both learned to love.
She wore a bell and was like angel from above.

&****&

He knew when to come into barn hearing her bell.
She nuzzled close to him and of her love she would tell.
They both had really great friend that pastured near them.
Their friend's name was Tina who they both thought a gem.

&***&

David never feared that Sunday was not happy.
Although they did not ride him he neighed real sappy.
Sue liked to groom him until his coat had nice shine.
It brought her back great memories that did remind.

&****&

Sunday would be happy in later years of life.
He was well taken care of and had little strife.
He was well cared for with respect and greatest love.
Sunday would be cherished as blessing from above.

&****&

The Fashion Show (Fable)

All the models were prepared to walk down the aisle.
For many it felt like walking nearly a mile.
All their hair had been arraigned to compliment them.
They all would wear a magnificent real rare gem.

&*****&

Lisa was the prettiest model I had seen.
Her attendant getting her ready was real mean.
She still needs the makeup to be put on just right.
In the back room she did hear two models in fight.

&****&

A man with camera opened dressing room door.
He smiled and then asked if she would pose on the floor.
He complimented her on how beautiful she did look.
He felt she would look great on cover of a book.

&****&

She posed and forgot that she did not even know him.
Then he left and things began to look really dim.
The jewels she was to wear could not even be found.
The man that took her picture was nowhere around.

&****&

The moral in this is not to be conceited.
The theft was a crime the person again repeated.
The model should not have been that concerned of looks.
She would be more valuable if she read more books.

&****&

The New Neighbor (Fable)

The new neighbor moved in just down the street.
They had two children that seemed quite neat.
The girl was a cheerleader, quite popular in school.
Her name was Alexis, and followed all the written rule.

&****&

The boy was quiet, and didn't have many friends at all.
He was a little small for his age, not very tall.
He was refused from football, as too small to play.
The coach did not want him, to get hurt in any way.

&****&

Matthew was very smart in school, better than all.
He did have some friends, not caring he was not tall.
He decided he wanted to have a career as a jockey.
He became famous, never had ever played hockey.

&*****&

The moral of this story is to be the best that you can.
Size does not matter, only if you learn how to stand.
Be good at what you do, whatever that may be.
Ask God for assistance, for the future you need to see.

&****&

Kitty Tales Part 13

My husband called at work telling me to come home.
Cat was hurt and he felt must not be home alone.
He heard a noise when he started the truck motor.
Mittens had been lying under hood near rotor.

&****&

Hank had heard the noise and had stopped it really fast.
The frightened shaken cat stopped meowing at last.
On the inner side of his legs was some dried blood.
The fur had to be shaved off along with the mud.

&****&

I left work and sped home fast on a rural road.
A truck leaving his yard hit me in reverse mode.
There was not much damage and I left driving slow.
I took down information as I did not know.

&****&

When I got home, we left to bring Mittens to Vet.
Diagnosis was miracle and not to fret.
I know we were lucky that he was doing fine.
If it had happened otherwise, I would lose mind.

&***&

Mittens was special kitty for surviving this.
He lived seventeen years of age and I do miss.
If you have a cat in cold months, do bang on hood.
Cats cuddle inside and we do not feel that they should.

&****&

Kitty Tales Part 14
Cuddles First Playmate

My daughter's fiancée bought her a Persian cat.
Named Serry, short for Serafim, imagine that!
He was tiny fluffy kitten with fur of grey.
My female Cuddles was happy, that's all I'll say.

&****&

Cuddles was only six months of age at the time.
She kept close to him, never further than a dime.
They became very good friends and would play all day.
Cuddles was happy until Serry moved away.

&****&

She would not look at my daughter, she was so mad!
She lost a piece of her heart, and was very sad.
Michelle did marry so Serry did leave our house.
I could not get Cuddles to play with her toy mouse.

&****&

We decided to get her another playmate.
We got a male she did learn to appreciate.
We named him Jake and Cuddles did learn to love him.
He liked to go out but I called him in when dim.

&****&

He was quite a character, loved the snacks I ate.
They played well together all day, it was their fate.
Cuddles was herself again and was quite happy.
They played like kittens together and got sappy.

&****&

The Greyhounds (Fable)

The greyhound dogs run races for prize money.
Often people, who do go, watch with their honey.
These dogs are quite tall, and sleek, and run very fast.
A good dog runs well, and a memory to last.

&****&

There was one certain greyhound that was very small.
He was called Colby, stocky but not very tall.
His owners thought maybe that they would let him race.
He did outstanding, taking the prize of first place.

&*****&

Colby was winner in any kind of weather.
His accomplishments are remembered forever.
He did not let size bother him in any way.
He just kept on trying his best, every day.

&*****&

The moral here is not to judge someone by size.
A foolish person does this, and this is not wise.
The smaller dog did what the larger could not.
Individual qualities can not be bought.

&****&

The Homeless Kitten

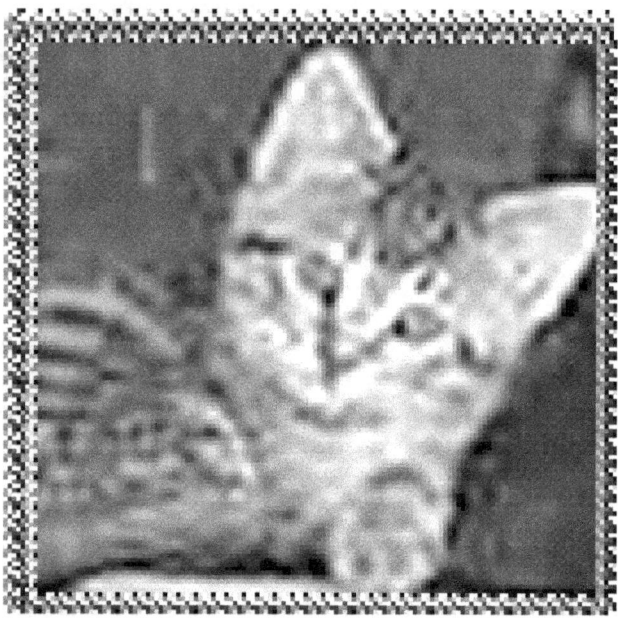

A small brown tiger kitten found himself in need.
His Mom pushed away as there were many to feed.
He then wandered off into the lush grassy field.
He is picked up by a Mother bunny and squealed.

&****&

She brings to her den and lays him beside her young.
She begins to wash him all over with her tongue.
He meows up at her and feels motherly love.
He fits perfect between the others like a glove.

&***&

Mother hare then decided to call cat Mittens.
He always was flexing his paws like most kittens.
She nursed with her own three bunnies and he did grow.
Soon he wondered why the others were very slow.

&****&

Mittens played hide and seek with Becky, Hank & Pat.
He was growing fast and quite spry not at all fat.
Soon he was going off on his own for his food.
He was good at it and came home in a good mood.

&***&

One day another large cat chased his brother Hank.
Mittens chased the cat away and then Hank did thank.
Their Mom was so proud that Mittens had protected.
She was thankful that his Mother had rejected.

&****&

Mittens lived here with them until he was a Dad.
He met a girl cat named Tammy that made him glad.
He promised to be close by to always protect.
He had been brought up with love and he would reflect.

&****&

The Llama

The oldest domestic animal is the llama.
They deliver one usually without much drama.
Their life span is about 15 to 25 years.
They are very social and do not have many fears.

&****&

They are known to chew their cud like cattle and our sheep.
They are used for many things and a good pet to keep.
They enjoy companionship of their species too.
They have calm nature and children can handle for you.

&****&

They are used for beast of burden and also a pet.
Their fur is used widely to make crafts without regret.
They are quite easy to train and they are very smart.
Their nature makes them pet you'll not want to be apart.

&****&

Weight can range between 300 and 400 pounds.
They're curious and browse around while making their rounds.
Their color can range from white to many shades of black.
They're six feet at head and around four around their back.

&****&

They have been found disease free and require little care.
They will spit if they are annoyed and then want to scare.
Adults don't ride but children enjoy ride on their back.
They can carry a lot of weight on back in a pack.

&****&

Kitty Tales Part 15
Magic's Summer Cut

My precious black cat Magic must be groomed each year.
His fur gets clumped together and it brings a tear.
As soon as warm weather arrives Hank does groom him.
Until he gets fur groomed his outlook is quite dim.

&****&

He has his own kit made for kitties and for dogs.
He is pretty good as I hold him, never sobs.
It takes two or three sessions before he is done.
Once he is finished, we let him out for some fun.

&****&

He gets real mushy and begins to wash his fur.
It grows back and hopefully clumps won't reoccur.
With all the clumps removed, he does feel much better.
I'm glad others don't get their fur stuck together.

&****&

The new fur will grow in very soft to the touch.
That is when I enjoy petting him very much.
After it is grown, he is gorgeous black cat.
I think he knows this and does strut imagine that!

&****&

Kitty Tales Part 16
Fluffy's Anxiety Attack

On Saturday mornings I had errands to do.
My cat Fluffy meowed fiercely as if she knew.
She was to have her kittens soon, so I let out.
I followed right after her and then I did shout.

&****&

One kitten was born as she tried to do her best.
Towels were placed under her so she could then rest.
She then did wash and I prayed to God to help her.
This was first heat and did not know what would occur.

&****&

I stayed with her for three hours as she cried in pain.
She had five kittens, four of which would be our gain.
One did not make it so we buried in the yard.
She was glad I stayed, even though for her was hard.

&****&

We found homes for two and then kept the other two.
These two brought companionship, of this I knew.
They were both tigers, named Tamatha and Mittens.
They were special as I saw birth, precious kittens.

&****&

I then brought them all in, preparing soft clean bed.
As she was the Mom, she then hid from me instead,
Spayed shortly after, there would not be any more.
After we took head counts as they went out the door.

&****&

I'm Randy the Robin

"I'm Randy the robin that lives in your backyard.
This is my mate Rose that knows when to make things hard.
You see, she is the ruler of our little home.
I follow her rules, otherwise will be alone.

&*****&

She knows when all the worms do come up from the grass.
While nesting, she does send me out to hunt with class.
I bring back her lunch, and she is a happy lass.
Sometimes there are many, and I find in great mass.

&****&

She keeps a watch when they put out some raisins too.
As she waits for our offspring, she has a great view.
Soon they will be born, and they will start to leave nest.
She knows when to teach them how to fly, she knows best.

&****&

For all you other birds out there, treat your mate right.
Those that play well will stay together, and not fight.
Otherwise you must get counsel form the wise owl.
Do not upset, and for sure she will never howl."

&****&

The Cardinal

If I was a bird, a cardinal I would be.
I would be a female and sing very sweetly.
I would be a good Mom and teach my young to fly.
I would keep them high in nest way up in the sky,

&****&

My mate would have to be strong, and good protector.
He would stand before us like a bright reflector.
If we were in danger, he would loudly cry out.
Each day we would hop together and all about.

&****&

I would harmonize with songbirds in the yard.
We might start off key, but later would not be hard.
Those that did not sing would hum along to the song.
We would sing loud if a strange flock did not belong.

&****&

Other birds would look and say we were a pretty pair.
I really think that we could not ever compare.
We would get along with most any other breed.
We kind of keep to ourselves unless we're in need.

&****&

Kitty Tales Part 17
Cuddles First Tumble Sault

Cuddles was black female cat that was ten years old.
She was a 12 pound kitty cat that was quite bold.
She never really cared to go outside at all.
She was content playing with Josh, they had a ball.

&****&

She was the older cat, and felt like she was his Mom.
He was neutered so he would not be a big tom.
They loved playing inside each and every day.
He also preferred the house, the outside no way.

&****&

Cuddles liked to sun herself in the window sill.
She captured hottest rays until she had her fill.
I didn't mind, as this way she was getting fresh air.
One day she knocked screen out, and tumbled out with care.

&****&

I had kitchen door open as was a nice day.
I heard loud frantic meows coming towards this way.
She had fallen from second floor and ran to door.
She does not sit in the windowsill any more.

&****&

I immediately let her in calming down.
She had run around the house meowing from ground.
I will close windows now when we are not at home.
I am afraid of what could happen if alone.

&****&

Kitty Tales Part 18
Cuddles Game of Hide and Seek

At this time Cuddles was only two pound kitten.
She crawled up my side stairs and I was just smitten.
It was the eve of a winter storm coming through.
I brought her in to feed as I knew I must do.

&****&

I placed in bathroom as I needed to train her.
She loved to sit in our lap and she would just purr.
If you raised your voice, she was afraid and would hide.
When we went to work, she was put in room inside.

&****&

In the bathroom she had her box, water and food.
When we came home, I then would open door to soothe.
One day I opened door and she was not in there!
I accused all of letting her out, what a scare!

&****&

We searched the room from the ceiling down to the floor.
We then heard meow coming from vanity door.
We opened up to find her curled up half asleep.
She opened door, slipped inside for a nap so neat!

&****&

After this I let her roam all around the house.
We bought her toys, the favorite the catnip mouse.
She hid for a while coming out only to eat.
As she got more confident, she followed for treat.

&****&

Gradually she gained trust, and would sit on our laps.
Her best time was when I read paper to relax.
Cuddles still does this whenever I try to read.
She will sit on paper when she feels she has need.

&****&

The Animal's Talent Show

On first day of summer; their talent show took place.
Many animals arrived with smile on their face.
Four trout would swim in the lake, like the dolphins do.
They were the first act and all did enjoy them too.

&*****&

The next act was Freddy the squirrel on the tree.
He was a furry acrobat for all to see.
A group of birds would sing a melody so fine.
Woody woodpecker played drums on tree so divine.

&*****&

The Goldfinch was the chorus as they sung so sweet.
The Blue jay stopped by but greedily took a treat.
Next act was three frogs hopping to beat of the drum.
The raccoon just watched enjoying as he did hum.

&****&

Sly the skunk came and he promised he would not spray.
He watched all acts in an appreciative way.
Some of them did clap in applause, but trout flipped high.
They all enjoyed this day with warm sun in blue sky.

&*****&

The rabbits were the last act of glorious day.
They and frogs played a game in an unusual way.
First bunny would jump over frog in beginning.
That frog jumped on bunny and then they were winning.

&*****&

That same bunny hopped over next frog and he joined.
The bunny played until had four frogs and then groined.
Then the frogs got off and the bunny felt relieved.
They had won the contest, never would have believed.

&****&

Kitty Tales Part 19

"Oh my, that skunk is drinking from my kitty dish.
I sincerely hope that he has made his last wish.
I sure hope that my Mom did wash that bad smell out.
Golly gee, she has just noticed him and did shout."

&****&

"Oh no, a small skunk is on the porch with the cat.
I will shut off the light and hope that does end that.
I will check later, hope Magic does keep away.
I sure do not want him smelly in nasty way."

&****&

"The light is out; I will just hide under the chair.
Finally she left the porch, has gone over there.
Gee it smells really rotten here, hope it's not me?
Mom will let me in, hope she does look out and see"

&****&

"Oh no, Magic you need a bath, you really smell!"
"Oops, Mom I do not think I am feeling quite well."
"Dad will give you a bath; now do close both your eyes."
"Well guess I smell good now, and now I am so wise."

&****&

"That skunk did look kind of attractive in the night.
I'll remember next time that will not bring delight.
Baths are for sissy cats, not for a male like me.
Mom, do I look like a stud now, please let me see."

&****&

Kitty Tales Part 20

Tale is of Tamatha and Mittens, two kittens.
Female named Tamatha and brother named Mittens.
My Daughter used to watch Samantha on Bewitched.
They were the greatest pair I would never have switched.

&***&

Michelle named Tamatha and that's what we called her.
She loved to play with them and pet their kitten fur.
After Mittens was neutered they had lots of fun.
They enjoyed outside and their adventures begun.

&***&

One day Mittens decided to climb up tall tree.
He meowed scared and then I finally did see.
Both Hank and I tried to persuade him to come down.
Hank then got out our tallest ladder with a frown.

&****&

While I talked to the cat Hank went up to get him.
His future outside at that time looked really dim.
We did not let him out until he was older.
When he was ready, he snuck out being bolder.

&****&

Tamatha was great hunter leaving gifts each day.
She loved being out having fun in her own way.
Both of these cats lived to be eighteen years of age.
We loved as young and when old at every stage.

&****&

Kitty Tales Part 21

This tale is about Cocoa and stray, named Midnight.
She was a young cat then, and found him a delight.
They went out together to play in our large yard.
It was easy to see, he had been her ace card.

&****&

They played together in our home every day.
You could not separate them, there was no way.
Cocoa was very happy she had a new friend.
She brought him home with her and they were friends till end.

&***&

They would not have kittens but would be a fine pair.
Their friendship was quite unique and none could compare.
Cocoa the female was sleek black and Bombay cat.
Midnight was a large black and white male, big not fat.

&****&

They were extremely happy playing throughout day.
Meowing happily was the way they did stay.
My Daughter bonded with him loving with her heart.
He slept beside her every night from the start.

&****&

This was only time these cats were ever apart.
Cocoa slept with me as I was love of her heart.
This was a fond memory I did have today.
Enjoy pets as someday they will be far away.

&****&

The Animal's Talent Show Part 2

On second day of talent show larger breeds came.
This day was when the larger showed skill through a game.
All were able to talk to each other in peace.
The bears showed all how they rid of itch and release.

&*****&

The large Grizzly bear scratched his back against pine tree.
Beaver mimicked to see if it would work for thee.
The beaver applauded as this surely was good.
This was what they would do rubbing up against wood.

&*****&

Two bucks would demonstrate without harm, deer in rut.
A small button buck did watch as they both did strut.
They came at each other as their antlers did wrap
All stepped back, so would not feel as if in a trap.

&*****&

Next was Ralph the raccoon and to the lake they went.
He did show how to wash food, and was heaven sent.
He explained importance of washing their hands too.
All animals that attended did not feel blue
.
&*****&

The birds had continued to sing sweet song to all.
Woody woodpecker was the drums, and doves wooing call.
The trout would flip up and down as the dolphins do.
This was how they applauded enjoyment of you.

&*****&

The frogs and bunnies continued as ending act.
All animals had enjoyed this, and that was fact.
Tomorrow all would be as it had been before.
Only in heaven this would be forevermore.

&****&

Kitty Tales Part 22

This is about two females Cocoa and Cuddles.
Cuddles was a tiny stray often in huddle.
Cocoa, the older cat was jealous from the start.
This really hurt me badly and did break my heart.

&****&

When I spent time with Cuddles, Cocoa got real mad.
When Cocoa was out, Cuddles was so very glad.
I believe Cocoa was around eight years of age.
If Cuddles was on my lap, Cocoa's eyes showed rage.

&***&

Mittens, a tiger male would then help Cuddles out.
He would defend kitten before I had to shout.
After a while then Cuddles grew bigger than she.
Then Cocoa stopped bothering her and let her be.

&****&

Cocoa the oldest girl was the Queen of the house.
She loved the outside and often caught a small mouse.
Cocoa was very possessive of all I love.
She is now precious angel from Heaven above.

&****&

Cuddles now is twelve whole pounds and precious to me.
She lives up to her name cuddling for all to see.
She is the Queen and her playmates are two large male.
They're Magic and Joshua and that's a new tale.

&****&

The Animal's Jamboree Part 3

The third day of summer couples came to the dance.
They arrived together and were happy to prance.
The Rumba was shown by the bears with lots of pride.
As their feet hit the ground many of them did hide.

&*****&

After each dance the trout did a flip in the lake.
They could not be in dance, but did want to partake.
The Chicken dance was done by the chickens on cue.
The many bird species sang some rock and roll too.

&****&

The frogs joined the bunnies to do the Bunny hop.
When they tired; trout entertained until told to stop.
The music had a nice beat although was quite hot.
Next Freddy fox and his mate showed all the Fox trot

&*****&

Woody woodpecker was great playing drums on tree.
Doves were chorus, finch and cardinal jamboree.
A pair of deer's was teaching all the Cha-Cha-Cha.
Other animals watched from either near or far.

&*****&

They all enjoyed this first week of summer the best.
After all the fun and games; they did need more rest.
The trout applauded and was last to bring delight.
Next week all would be normal and most out of sight.

&****&

Kitty Tales Part 23

"Meow, it is time to go outside to catch mice.
If we catch a few, Mom will think we are real nice.
I love to make her happy; she'll hug me all night.
Show her what we caught; do not take even small bite."

&****&

"Look Tammy, a chipmunk I do see over there."
"No, No, last time she got mad as if she did care."
"Oh, all right; I will not go after him to kill.
I will just play with it increasing my great skill."

&****&

"Golly gee Mittens; look at the big cat near barn.
He does not look like he settles to play with yarn."
Don't worry Tammy, we can just go on inside.
I do not want to fight him; so let us just hide."

&****&

Looking from window; they watch the cat leave in style.
They'll stay in a bit and then go out for a while.
"Tammy be glad I did not have a fight with him."
"Of course, I would rather you exercise at gym."

&****&

"Mom always says it is best not to fight at all.
It is better to talk things out, that is best call.
Now that we're in, how about playing with the yarn?
"Sure as long as it's not the one she uses to darn."

&****&

Kitty Tales Part 24

Cuddles was kitten when Michelle got Persian cat.
He was a gift from her betrothed, imagine that
Michelle called her male grey fluffy kitten, Serry.
Together Cuddles and Serry were quite merry.

&****&

They often would play tag around the entire house.
They even did take turns playing with catnip mouse.
They were inseparable happy each new day.
They were happy until Michelle had moved away.

&****&

Of course, her cat Serry did go to his new home.
Cuddles had been left and was upset and alone.
She remains mad at my Daughter until present.
Only after she had friend, she became pleasant.

&****&

Serry now has Amber as his new female friend.
Amber is a female Persian, buddy till end.
Now Serry has Amber, and Cuddles has her Josh.
Now all of our felines are ecstatic, by gosh!

&****&

Now Cuddles has two playmates, and both she finds dear.
If they are ever separated, she'll shed tear.
Daily, Magic and Joshua get along well.
Magic told Josh of the skunk and the horrid smell.

&****&

A Bird's Flight

I am a large hawk and fly around well.
I keep my eyes alert for chicks that fell.
I'm fast when I see food for my table.
I will hunt until I am not able.

&****&

Small animals make the best meal ever.
I hunt well in any kind of weather.
I will mate to keep my breed very strong.
I will teach my young to hunt before long.

&****&

I usually sit on a tree and wait.
A snake may be seen and then lose to fate.
Small mice in a cornfield may be my snack.
Crayfish are real tasty and I may attack.

&****&

I sometimes will hunt with up to six hawks.
They will flush prey from brush while others stalk.
Some will watch for predators of our breed.
Others will watch to help the hunt succeed.

&****&

My mate lays two or three eggs per season.
Nest must be high, protection the reason.
Coyotes have been known to pull down nest.
We try hard to protect as do the rest.

&****&

I'm Sam the Squirrel

"I'm Sam the squirrel and this is Sara my mate.
I chose her and I really do appreciate.
We found this country home where we can run and play.
Breakfast is under the pines, what more can I say?

&*****&

They bought us a squirrel table, imagine that!
Up there, we have better view of Magic the cat.
It is really cool and looks like stump of a tree.
Cracked corn comes out of each side for Sara and me.

&****&

Just a little note Mom, don't keep it always full.
My excited Sara eats too much as a rule.
She needs to trim down a little as she is fat.
I do not want her to be the next meal for cat.

&****&

Come on Sara, it is time for me to chase you.
I'm starting to feel frisky, and hope you are too.
Well guess what, I think you have had enough to eat.
Let us play, as I will be giving you a treat."

&****&

The Stray Cat

A stray cat, black with white throat did appear.
Hungry he approached a lumberjack near.
He meowed at the man and he fed him.
The thankful cat knew future was not dim.

&****&

The man seemed to be a friendly fellow.
He did not pick fights and seemed quite mellow.
He enjoyed the cat and named him Midnight.
By campfire someone always threw delight.

&****&

He was well fed and slept in tent with Dan.
Dan loved the cat and Midnight loved this man.
One day a tiny chipmunk was in camp.
It was raining and poor thing was so damp.

&***&

**Midnight picked him up and brought inside tent.
The chipmunk was scared and thought he'd repent.
Midnight meowed telling him he wouldn't harm.
The chipmunk felt he had found lucky charm.**

&**&**

**The sun came up and Midnight brought him food.
He was starving and this really did soothe.
He thanked Midnight and became his good friend.
Chris the chipmunk did hope this would not end.**

&**&**

**Chris found shelter for his family here.
There was always lots of food that was dear.
Midnight enjoyed talking with all of them.
They treasured his friendship, thought him a gem.**

&**&**

Kitty Tales Part 25

Magic is my black indoor-outdoor kitty cat.
At weight of sixteen pounds he is really quite fat.
He's treasure having a great personality.
He often blinks saying, "I love you" sincerely.

&****&

He lies near as we mulch the trees and flower bed.
He often will come near us to butt with his head.
You can pick him up, and hold him outside or in.
He lets you pet him, looking up as if you're kin.

&****&

Anyone can pet him; he will not scratch or bite.
He will only act this way if he had a fight.
He's not a tom cat now, so stays around the house.
Many times he's in driveway as he eats a mouse.

&****&

He gets along with two other cats in my home.
He's comfortable being outside, does not roam.
In winter, he may play with the female a while.
She has two playmates now, always has a big smile.

&****&

He probably was owned before he came to us.
He is precious, as all humans he now does trust.
With personality, I am very impressed.
For this reason, I feel he's my absolute best.

&****&

Kitty Tales Part 26

The grandfather clock chimed each hour of entire day.
My house cats found it annoying, in their own way.
The first time they heard, they scattered so very fast!
It was humorous; I wish that it could have last.

&***&

It took a while for them to get used to the chime.
I purposely watched if in kitchen at that time.
As with doorbell, they later did not really care.
Meanwhile every time it rang, they got a scare.

&****&

Both of these cats would never survive in the wild.
They both do remind me of a frightened small child.
Joshua I taught to have fear of a loud thing.
I chased with a vacuum and a scare I did bring.

&***&

I did this because Jake had been killed by a car.
I had called him home, as he never went quite far.
He always would run to me when he heard my voice.
Different this time, calling him had been bad choice.

&****&

Now Josh and Cuddles are just my two inside cats.
The worse they'll do are having own play sneak attacks.
Magic is only cat that goes out and is brave.
Although neutered protects his turf and is engaged.

&****&

Kitty Tales Part 27

My name is Fluffy and I am a young kitty.
My first home is with a family in the city.
I am fluffy angora, grey with paws of white.
I am not their first pet, but surely a delight.

&****&

They have these two pets that are in a cage.
I like to stare at them and then they do enrage.
My owner's daughter named Mary and Rose.
They smell like a good dinner by my nose!

&****&

They are guinea pigs, and they love them too.
Golly since I came; all they do is eat and poo!
Maybe I might be able to unlatch their door.
Mom just noticed me beside them on the floor.

&*****&

"Fluffy, get away, you are giving them a scare."
"Really Ma, do you really think I might care."
Oh well; best listen or there will be no fish food.
I will rub her leg, then she will be in good mood.

&****&

Well tomorrow; I will try to play with Mary.
She looks like large black rat and is real scary.
At least my name describes what I look like.
Named after Aunts, must want to take a hike.

&****&

Kitty Tales Part 28

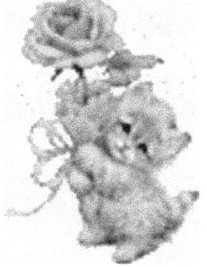

"When I was a small kitty, Mom placed me here.
I was inside something furry, but she was near.
She keeps making me walk inside with chicken.
It is really good so I will, as it is paw licking.

&****&

I think I like this cat tree she bought for me.
I am small and climb to top, and wow can I see!
Great, there is this furry mouse on top here too.
Oh, this is lots of great fun for me and also you.

&****&

As a wee kitten, I just want to tell Mom thanks.
I promise that I will not do too many pranks.
This is great; there is room for three more of us.
I do not believe that it will fall, in Mom I trust.

&****&

I think they buy this, because we need exercise.
Mom, you didn't waste your dough, you are wise.
I promise to work out here, each and every day.
Meow, Mom do you understand what I did say?

&****&

I think I had enough exercise for this first day.
I want to see if more chicken will come my way.
Listen up you felines, play dumb a short while.
You pretend, and chicken will then be your style."

&****&

The Wood Ducks

The wood ducks make their nest by forest stream.
It is up to us to keep water clean.
You will see them fishing for breakfast too.
They continue when unaware of you.

&****&

Smart ducks know when to fish from the ocean.
They fish as you put on suntan lotion.
Their tail feathers are violet and blue.
Their body is brown and they're pretty view.

&****&

Mother teaches babies to swim while small.
They swim beside and feel Mom is quite tall.
Mother protects from all that would cause harm.
They sense when danger is near with alarm.

&****&

Treat all wildlife areas with great care.
Respect their environment; be aware.
Cleanliness is next to Godliness too.
Keeping their home clean will make things look new.

&****&

Wildlife land needs to be protected well.
People need to spread the word and to tell.
With their homes pristine; their breeds will be strong.
Forest cleanliness does always belong.

&****&

The Magical Kingdom

The magical kingdom was home to many creatures.
The stream's water was one of its best features.
After drinking it, all felt the presence of peace.
There was no prey here, just a sense of release

&****&

Not one animal ever felt hunger living here.
They lived in harmony and existence was dear.
There were males and females of each breed.
The males did not fight, here all did succeed.

&*****&

There were tropical birds here as it was warm.
If predators were seen; they would do no harm.
There was a pretty rainbow up high in the sky.
Different bird types drank, and flew on by.

&****&

The animals could talk to each other every day.
They enjoyed life here, and glad they could stay.
There was friendship for all, unlike any other place.
Here all had peace and did not fear another's face.

&*****&

There is a place like this where our pets do reside.
They live happily and do not fear or have to hide.
Their kingdom is in heaven right at the garden gate.
They will run happily to greet us when it is our fate.

&****&

Kitty Tales Part 29

"I'm Magic, a black inside-outside kitty cat.
Mom was feeding birds and saw me, imagine that.
I only stay inside when it gets too cold out.
When inside, I like to chase cute Cuddles about.

&****&

She's fine female I would love to snuggle down with.
They have neutered me and darn; I still want to live!
Well spring is soon, as I am shedding my thick fur.
I hope when I am outside that no fights do occur.

&****&

The last two nights I slept in the porch rocker chair.
Mom checks often and I guess she really does care.
She lets me inside in the middle of the night.
It's always great to have a snack, a real delight.

&****&

Mischief can be brewing; I must find others.
Joshua knows I am boss cat, we're best brothers.
He's my opposite, likes to sit in a window sill.
He prefers staying in; I guess that's his free will.

&****&

I must find sister Cuddles, maybe we can play?
Oh darn; she is asleep snoring in her own cute way.
I guess I'll crash on the top perch of kitty tree.
I can see that no one is up there, and it's calling me."

&****&

Kitty Tales Part 30

"My names Cuddles, and thought it was time for my tale.
I know you'll enjoy more than one of the small whale.
I followed female cat home on a wintry day.
Deserted as not perfect, what more can I say?

&****&

This cat was Cocoa and hated me in her home.
I hid when they worked, and we kitties were alone.
She was so jealous when Mom showed me any love!
I knew I needed guidance from God up above.

&****&

When I got bigger; she stopped pushing me around.
When I weighed as much as her, she acted like clown.
I really prefer the house, as I've known trauma.
Vet said someone hit my eye, I had known drama.

&****&

We did not get along so Mom bought me playmate.
Jake and I bonded and I did appreciate.
He liked to go out and I missed when he left me.
I watched from sill at all the birds and scenery.

&****&

He was few months older than me, and we had fun.
We chased each other as soon as day begun.
I did love him and I will remember all our time.
He was killed crossing street, driver was past their prime.

&****&

The Sheep Family (Fable)

The sheep herd was protected by a Border collie.
She protected from wolves, her name was Mollie.
There was Sam, the Dad, and Sara the Mom.
Their kids were Sheila and of course son, Tom.

&*****&

Mollie was great at keeping the wolves away.
She would guard all of them well, night and day.
The wolves would very much like to eat the sheep.
Mollie was a great guard dog; farmer would keep.

&****&

Mollie was sick one day, and did not get to guard.
The lead sheep had to keep together, it was hard.
Tom started to fool that he saw wolves near.
All of the flock scattered, all over in fear.

&****&

Sara told Tom never to play silly game to fool.
It was not right to upset all, that was a good rule.
He did listen to his Mom, but did so once more.
Sam told him to stop, or he would push through door.

&*****&

Mollie was still not well, flock was left alone.
Tom decided to play a game, off did roam.
He needed help, the wolves gathered all around.
He yelled for help falling to the ground.

&*****&

The other sheep thought he was playing a game.
They just laughed and shouted out his name.
The moral is to never lie for no one will trust.
You must always tell the truth, this is a must.

&****&

The Raccoon's Dilemma

"Oh darn, looks like tonight I do not get fed.
I was hoping to have a full tummy for bed.
I do not know why the birds do not share.
I am only one raccoon, if only they would care.

&****&

I guess I will go down to the next house.
Golly gee, I think I just stepped on a mouse.
Better luck next time pal, I am bigger than you.
I hope I find some food soon or I will feel blue.

&*****&

I will definitely be back here tomorrow night.
I am sure they know I must eat by daylight.
I am careful not to disturb as they're asleep.
My claws are loud, only if there's no food to eat."

&****&

The Turtle and the Hare (Fable)

Teddy turtle and Henry hare were friends a while.
The hare decides to have race of quarter of a mile.
Turtle thought he'd comply, although he knew he was slow.
The other animals watched, then someone said, "Go."

&*****&

Both Teddy and Henry did start out for the race.
Henry took a short cut so he would not lose face.
Oops, there was a problem; a cat was on this path.
Henry was scared now, did not want to cause any wrath.

&******&

Teddy looked behind him, but did not see the hare.
Teddy looked in front and still no hare anywhere.
Teddy just kept on walking, as fast as he could.
He was having a good time, as he knew he would.

&*****&

Meanwhile; Henry hid behind bush quiet as a mouse.
He felt very bad, wished he had stayed at his house.
Finally the cat had left, and he started out.
He got back on the right road to hear a loud shout.

&*****&

Up ahead he sees that Teddy crossed the finish line.
He did fail and certainly he did not feel fine.
The moral is be honest in what you may do.
Honesty's best, and will be successful for you.

&****&

Kitty Tales Part 31

"My name is Cuddles, and I have a story to tell.
I need to get Mom's attention like a warning bell.
I will meow weird, so she will come into room.
There's a fox outside, and do not want Magic's doom."

&****&

"Sweet Cuddles what is wrong, I will be right there."
She then glanced outside and saw a real scare.
There was a red fox eating corn from feeder she bought.
She needed to find Magic before he was caught.

&****&

She ran and opened porch door and was quite relieved
Magic ran inside, knowing danger I had perceived."
"I was grateful Cuddles had given me warning note.
I would have known by clumps of fur on his black coat."

&****&

"This episode was one I will never forget.
I'm glad I paid attention, I have no regret.
Pay attention whenever your pets act strange.
Get up at once to find out reason for the change."

&*****&

"Cuddles Mom loves you so much for this act of love.
Magic knows that his home is a gift from above."
"Lastly Mom needs to spend more time with all of us.
Now I feel I have showed her this, of this I trust."

&****&

Kitty Tales Part 32

Near our pellet stove the cats will often soundly sleep.
They enjoy warmth it brings and feel it is really neat.
At times; Josh sits in front of it watching the flames.
Then suddenly they get playing at one of their games.

&****&

He is fascinated to see flames flicker from glass door.
It almost hypnotizes, and then he will curl up on floor.
They miss in the spring when we no longer have it on.
I did find them sleeping in front of, in the early morn.

&****&

Now they're happy when they sit in the window sill.
They sit there with soft breeze as they do get their fill.
It brings out their feelings usually in a frisky manner.
They run after each other as tails are high as a banner.

&****&

They enjoy watching the birds from their window seat.
They each have own sill and watch them on suet treat.
They see the fat squirrel eat his ear of corn on the cob.
They are usually in their seats when I leave for my job.

&****&

Cuddles and Josh enjoy themselves throughout the day.
I know they appreciate the feeders I do have on display.
They are content to stay in house and watch each scene.
When I come home; they are happy meowing and serene.

&****&

The Squirrel Family

There was Sammy and Sherry, the Ma and the Pa.
Their nest was on top of a pine tree, very far.
They had two little ones, a small girl and a boy.
They were quite happy together and had much joy.

&****&

They came down from the tree very early to eat.
They enjoyed the sunflower seeds, a special treat.
Sherry warned them to be real watchful of the cat.
He found them a delight, even though were not fat.

&****&

They grew to adults, then Magic felt them fair game.
He enjoyed playing tag, often calling them by name.
Sherry kept warning not to listen, he'll trick you.
The cat did corner and kill, making his Ma blue.

&****&

Sammy warned Sara, listen we always know best.
If Sly had listened he would not now be at rest.
As a parent, our experience best guides you.
Respect warnings and all will go well with you too.

&****&

Life as a Bear

This is a story about Ben and Betty bear.
Ben did really like her company, he did care.
He did love to watch her hunt, almost every day.
He knew she was really special in her own way.

&*****&

They spent time together and she would be a Mom.
She did hope to have two cubs, one would be called Tom.
She knew she would be wise and great as a Mom.
She was a very wise bear, never was called dumb.

&****&

She had a boy and a girl that means she had two.
She was very happy now, never ever was blue.
Ben did stray away after both cubs had been born.
Betty did not care, was real happy and not forlorn.

&***&

The cubs would learn hunting staying with her a while.
This is the way it is with bears, it is their style.
She would teach how to survive finding food to eat.
They did listen and then she would give them a treat.

&****&

When grown to adults, they would go off on their own.
She might come across them in territory they roam.
Another large male would look for her soon.
She felt it was time now, beautiful full moon.

&****&

The Giraffe Family (Fable)

There were two giraffes, Gladys and Gene.
They were both in love, neither was mean.
They had two young, a girl and a boy.
This brought them happiness and great joy.

&****&

The girl was called Glory and the boy Gus.
They played together always, that was a must.
Glory was beautiful, precious to the breed,
Gus was far smaller in size, in great need.

&****&

Gus felt very bad that he was so small.
He could not run as fast to catch the ball.
At times, the taller ones did constantly tease him.
He decided to show them by going to a gym.

&****&

Mom then told him to eat all the right food.
He began to grow taller, changing his mood.
Eating right, exercise and sleep, Mom said he needed.
He became taller and quite handsome, had succeeded.

&****&

The moral is to trust in what your parents say.
They have been around a lot more than a day.
They will teach you to grow up in the best way.
Remember their wisdom is like warmth of sun's ray.

&****&

Kitty Tales Part 33

This is about Joshua, a grey and white male.
Biblical name we gave to protect what prevail.
He is nervous cat, very high strung at all times.
He ever feared the Grandfather clocks hourly chimes.

&****&

He is tallest of the three cats that we do own.
He has beautiful facial markings if was shown.
His appearance is slightly longer and real sleek.
He is good sized male but very timid and meek.

&****&

The highlight of his day is to play hide and seek.
They're playmates always reaching their happiness peak.
He is fascinated by all moths that may sneak in.
He will jump the highest and it then is din-din.

&****&

I should have named Grasshopper, this name is unique.
He is barrel of laughs as he hides taking peek.
He is my angel, always senses when I'm sick.
As inside cat, I do not worry of a tick.

&****&

They're all precious paw prints on my hearts which I love.
They are great gifts given to me by God above.
I do treasure every day I play with each.
They love in all moods, not like people you can't reach.

&****&

Kitty Tales Part 34

This story's about the playfulness of a cat.
My two inside are playmates until they have spat.
Their new toy has suction cups that stick to the floor.
When we come home; it's lying sideways near the door.

&****&

Cuddles gave us fine demonstration just last night.
She would swat hard and it would then twirl with delight.
Next she lay on floor near it and played with the string.
She was telling us she enjoyed her new plaything.

&****&

When they tire of toys; they enjoy a bottle cap.
They play ferociously, like they're doing a rap.
If I misplace a button; I can forget that.
I will find it later under carpet or mat.

&****&

These cats are grown but I like to treat as before.
I feel they'll live longer and love me even more.
My Cuddles is probably eleven years old.
My husband bought Josh at pet shop where he was sold.

&****&

Joshua was only one ever bought for me.
All others followed cats home and were always free.
All these strays became part of loving family.
They opened their hearts and all loved me sincerely.

&****&

Kitty Tales Part 35

"I'm Magic the cat, and I live in country home.
I was a stray, but now I am never alone.
I'm the only cat that likes to hunt and goes out.
Often Mom gets mad when I hunt and she does shout.

&*****&

I have Brother Josh and a sister named Cuddles.
They don't go out, especially if there's puddles.
It's a big deal if they get paws a little wet.
They don't even know what a mouse is, never met.

&*****&

Yeah if you did not know; I'm the biggest male cat.
I might have to lose some as the Vet says I'm fat.
It would rather stay this way, look huge to others.
Mom is great and I don't want any more brothers.

&*****&

Hey Mom, do you have some time to really groom me?
My fur is getting clumpy again, I can see.
The weather is getting hot too and I get sticky.
It does not have to be perfect; I'm not picky.

&*****&

There is this girl kitty down the street that I like.
She snubbed me as I looked, and told me take a hike.
It is not good for my image to look like this.
I promise to be still so not one clump you'll miss."

&****&

The Unicorn Family

Animals in the enchanted forest did thrive.
Here all lived in harmony and all did survive.
Ursula was Mom and Ulysses was the Dad.
Uri was their son that made them both very glad.

&****&

They often took children up high for little ride.
They had great personalities they could not hide.
If children had fear, they would prance just off the ground.
Their hoofs were a soft gallop and a pleasant sound.

&****&

Visitors could feed them their special homemade treat.
They enjoyed home here always having lots to eat.
Being able to talk to humans was just great.
All kiddies especially did appreciate.

&****&

Of all animal rides unicorns were the best!
They could take them high in the sky not like the rest.
Thumbelina was fun because of her small size.
Parents thought babies would enjoy and they were wise.

&****&

All that were given a ride held on to their horn.
Sometimes turkeys went for a ride to get to corn.
The corn field was quite a ways for turkeys to walk.
When they rode on unicorns, they often would talk.

&****&

Although turkeys can fly they enjoyed the ride too!
They really enjoyed when skies were beautiful blue.
The unicorns were all white and a pleasure to see.
They had the finest beauty they ever could be.

&****&

The Dragon Family

The dragon family was never at all stressed.
The fire they would blow was always urgent request.
Campers would always ask dragons to start their fire.
All stood back while Dan and Doreen brought flames higher.

&****&

The dragons were happy now that they had Denise.
They were good dragons living in forest in peace.
The Enchanted forest was their home and quite grand.
They could talk to all the animals and to man.

&****&

They offered rides to all that visited within.
They cared for one another as if they were kin.
Sometimes the dragons and the unicorns would race.
All that did watch from the ground would often embrace.

&****&

Dan and Doreen were working on their own dance step.
They looked into each other eyes hopping with pep.
Then they bounced their tails up and down, then all around.
They moved around quite swiftly as they stomped the ground.

&****&

All that watched it thought they would try the Dragon stroll.
All the others began to practice on the knoll.
Those that had no tails would loudly stomp both their feet.
It was cute to watch partners as they did repeat.

&****&

In Enchanted forest the dragons were just swell.
Riding on them was so much fun and all would tell.
All were harnessed in as skin was scaly to hold.
Thinking back on memories was great to behold.

&****&

The Donkey's Story

A donkey wanted to be known in history.
When he was born, his Mother knew this was to be.
Donkey carried Mary to Town of Bethlehem.
Here Jesus was born to be Savior of men.

&****&

He had carried the most precious cargo of all.
Among all his peers, this donkey stood very tall.
The King of Kings was born with animals around.
His first cry was surrounded by animal sound.

&****&

This was to teach all animals can have great worth.
From the littlest to the largest, they all have mirth.
Jesus was born in a stable with those that loved him.
It is to him we must turn when things look quite dim.

&****&

Not all donkeys have an important role as this.
All animals should be cared for with love and bliss.
From his beginning Jesus taught us to respect.
All creatures in our care we must never neglect.

&****&

The poorest of homes can be the happiest place.
It is how we live that can bring smiles to our face.
In beginning life began with great deal of love.
If we nurture this, it will be blessed from above.

&****&

This donkey lived life and important destiny.
He did help fulfill prophesy as is should be.
When you see a donkey, do remember this tale.
Your spirit will then be uplifted without fail.

&****&

Kitty Tales Part 36
The Mischievous Kittens

"Tammy, do you want to know how we can have fun?"
He unrolls the toilet paper, it had begun.
They both had a great time now that it was undone.
"He tags Tammy then; see how fast you now can run?"

&****&

"Oh alright, I will get you back really quite soon."
Then they played tag, she was able to catch at noon.
"Mittens, let's go eat some of Mom's leafy plant."
"Oh, I do not think we should, she may rave and rant."

&****&

"Are you afraid, she'll not know if it's you or me?"
"Oh, lets do it; I'm mischievous as can be."
Then they both eat most of the leaves from her new rose.
They enjoyed scent and would sniff the rose with their nose.

&*****&

They slept for couple of hours, awoke to a car.
"Quick scatter Tammy, Mom can not be very far."
They both scattered and ran every way now.
I opened the door then but I felt that somehow...

&*****&

I went to the bathroom and saw it was all messed.
I must laugh now but at the time felt not blessed.
"Tammy and Mittens, I know now what you have done!
There will be no more of this mischief my precious ones."

&****&

A Calico Named Patches

"I'm Patches and I'm female Calico kitty.
I reside with Mom in country home in city.
I am mostly inside cat, but like exercise.
Mom got baby chicks as playmates, although not wise.

&*****&

They were little; I had to get a better look.
They were on house floor and I went near, and Mom shook.
They all seem to be growing bigger in their pen.
I started to chase them but my Mom yelled again.

&*****&

Gee whiz, I just wanted to play with them a bit.
I don't know why she gets upset, and takes a fit.
Now looks like Mom and Dad are making place outside.
Golly they were just learning how to play inside.

&****&

I hope she gets me mate to amuse during day.
Squeaky toys are stupid, that is all I can say.
Mom don't throw bottle cap out, I can toss about.
I got it; she just noticed and started to shout.

&****&

Guess I better watch fish in aquarium swim.
Life is not exciting to me, it is quite dim.
While they're working, I really need to play real hard.
You can let me out, I promise to stay in yard."

&****&

ﺵKitty Tales Part 37

"My name is Joshua and I have tale to tell.
I had to wake Mom today as she was not well.
The loud alarm was playing for nearly an hour.
I wanted to eat, and then she could take shower.

&****&

I climbed onto her chest and kneaded quite gently.
She did not wake up, so I did differently.
I lay on top of her back, and then I stretched out.
It did not take long; she woke up and then did shout."

&****&

"Ok I'm getting up now; I guess you need food."
She then went downstairs, and did seem in better mood.
She put on coffee, and a smile came to her face.
Mom let Magic in, and then we all had a race.

&****&

Magic pushed through me and my Sister Cuddles now.
Mom looks at Magic funny and raised her eyebrow.
There were grey dove feathers on the porch on the mat.
"I wish you'd wait until I feed you, you bad cat!"

&****&

We had filet mignon in house, what a darn shame!
Mom knows it was not me; it's Magic she will blame.
I don't understand why he must go out and kill.
He does not have to show us that he has great skill."

&****&

ش‌Kitty Tales Part 38

"My names Magic and this is me telling story.
Mom's pet squirrel passed, and now has seen glory.
I saw him as he lie in middle of street.
Dad placed him in forest across which was real neat.

&****&

I felt that Mom should know so I then did retrieve.
I placed in her flower bed so she could grieve.
Dad notices and told Mom I put squirrel there.
Mom goes out and picks up, and shows all she did care."

&****&

"Thanks Magic for bringing this to my attention.
If only we had taught him hazard prevention."
"They would go back and forth planting seed across.
Now the poor little squirrel his life has been lost.

&****&

Thanks Dad for clipping that huge fur ball that's back there.
Golly gee, my mirror image was horrid scare!
Now I will get brushed and then pet with lots of love.
My prayers were answered; God did hear me above.

&****&

Now that I wrote this; I must go outside to play.
There are a few black birds out, and one might stray.
If I have more adventures; I will tell you soon.
I hear lots of chattering, they're playing my tune."

&****&

Kitty Tales Part 39

"My name is Magic, and I am a black male cat.
I'm not tomcat now, but it's better to be fat.
I have very thick black fur and these big green eyes.
I was outside cat before, so they say I'm wise.

&****&

I stumbled across this yard and knew I found home.
Mom and Dad took me in and now I'm not alone.
There's a sweet female here by the name of Cuddles.
She lets me play with her, but she never snuggles.

&****&

There's another male here, tuxedo black and white.
My brother's name's Joshua and we do not fight.
He knows I am the boss of this country domain.
Since I arrived, neither cat has been quite the same.

&****&

They play together only when I'm not in game.
I can be ferocious, so these two are real tame.
They are both content just being within the house.
They do not even know the scent of a real mouse!

&****&

They're happy to play with catnip mouse on the floor.
As soon as I wake, I meow to go out door.
I'm loved and given attention, even a treat.
Yippee, heard the can opener, its time to eat!

&****&

I'll take a nap afterwards all stretched out somewhere.
I nap on the bed, sometimes in the rocking chair.
When I sleep, sometimes I remember a new tale.
If I do not, they come up with one without fail."

&****&

Tinniesville Part 1

Tinniesville was a small rural town in the dell.
It was named after midgets far as I can tell.
All that did reside here would help one another.
There was no hatred all treated as your brother.

&****&

They used the barter system to obtain their wealth.
Doctors would attend sick when they were in ill health.
After well they then assisted Doctor when needed.
He might help with crop that needed to be seeded.

&****&

The children got along well playing with their pets.
They loved their animals, there were never regrets.
Babies were given rides on the larger dog breeds.
Seamstress's and tailors made clothes for all their needs.

&****&

The baker cooked for all the birthday parties too.
His fee was then paid when errands were run by you.
Church was open to all to worship together.
Come rain or shine all attended in all weather.

&****&

There was no jealously among all that lived here.
They were noted for many types of hats quite dear.
People from nearby towns stopped here to buy a hat.
There was big business in hats, imagine that!

&****&

Some came here to see the magicians and great clowns.
Not one person ever would wear sad face or frowns.
Others came to see" The Princess and her Prince Play."
There were many attractions, that's all I can say.

&****&

The visitors do not judge midgets for their size.
They feel size means nothing as they are all real wise.
Here all show their friendship and treat all with respect.
It's a great place to visit and to then reflect.

&****&

Tinniesville #2

The town's mayor was a well respected teacher.
He opened each day with prayer from the preacher.
He kept all of them interested with the arts.
At recess they even were able to throw darts.

&****&

He felt education was important to all.
He even taught poetry to those that had call.
As he could write and paint portraits, he taught this too.
He was good with depression for those that were blue.

&****&

Math, History and English were learned by all there.
His great knowledge in these things, he often would share.
Those in town that had talent would teach the others.
Magic and actors taught their sisters and brothers.

&***&

People from Heathersville began to visit here.
The two towns had attractions that were very dear.
The town would have joint picnic and get together.
They especially visited in spring weather.

&****&

There was always entertainment for someone too.
Peace would come over all that saw Heathersviille view.
Midgets went to the Hot spring for healing effect.
They then grew normal size without any regret.

&****&

Their entire family then joined in the hot springs.
They then built in the dale and brought all of their things.
Some of the midgets did not care about their size.
They were used to being small and felt they were wise.

&****&

Tinniesville Part Three

Those midgets that grew were sorry they had changed fate.
They missed their community and became irate
They went back to spring wishing they were as before.
They dried themselves off and their clothes fell to the floor.

&****&

They would move back to Tinnesville and be happy.
The first midget arriving was now a pappy.
He would teach children to be content with their looks.
Their lives could be great as long as they learned from books.

&***&

They would teach all that size is not important too.
It is more important the good things that you do.
It is the person inside that really matters.
Don't judge by clothes either fancy or in tatters.

&****&

Examine your conscience to find out who you are.
It may take a while and you may travel quite far.
Once you realize potential do this work well.
Your face will show happiness and glow that will tell.

&****&

Pastures sometimes look greener on the other side.
It is best to be yourself and never to hide.
Look in mirror knowing you are best you can be.
Pray to God daily and benefits you will see.

&****&

Kitty Tales Part 40

"Golly I'm so glad Mom came out to warm up car.
It's really cold out, I'm glad I did not go far.
I guess I'll snack, then go on kitty tree for nap."
"What is going on down there, it sounds like a rap?

&*****&

"Oh, it's just Cuddles and Josh playing in the hall."
"Keep it down guys; just wake me up for your meal call!
Oh, such sweet dreams I really do have way up here!
Here I can lie on my back with nothing to fear.

&****&

I will have to see what joy they do find with that?
It seems that they are batting around a toy, that's fact.
Oh these toys that Mom does buy have such a great scent!
I feel frisky and my energy is well spent.

&*****&

That's why Josh and Cuddles were so active before,
Mom thank you for buying this, you really do score!
For all you strays, it's best to find a family.
A family cares for you with sincerity.

&****&

I used to have to fight someone, just to survive.
Now I am well fed and thank God I'm still alive.
They took care of me when I got hurt from a fight.
Now I'm just a big black kitty that feels delight.

&*****&

Sorry I did forget to tell you who I am.
My name's Magic and my family is just grand.
All we cats are born writers, and tales we do tell.
I really laughed learning how sweet Cuddles had fell."

Till next time," Meow"

&****&

Kitty Tales Part 41

This tale is about my husband's Grammas' kitty.
He was a male Siamese and he lived in the city.
Sebastian became hard for her to care for.
We had a kitten so we thought, what is one more?

&*****&

So she gave him to us and we took him home.
I was afraid to leave little Fluffy alone.
When we brought him home, we brought him in the kitchen.
Fluffy was so nervous, she was just twitching.

&****&

We knew we could not keep so we put in the cellar.
I gave Hank food and he went to feed the big fellar.
As he stooped to put the food down, the cat did jump!
He climbed on top of his back with claws ka-plunk!

&****&

Hank then did scream for me to get him off his back.
His claws drew blood as he dug them in to attack.
We then came upstairs afterwards, quite upset.
Morning could not come fast enough, was it light yet?

&****&

We then brought him back to her the very next day.
"Oh" He did not open the door;" She then did say.
It seems he was so smart he knew how to turn knob.
I'm glad he was not home when we were at our job!

&****&

The Raccoon

The raccoon washes all food it intends to eat.
They often eat from our birdfeeders for a treat.
They are usually nocturnal, and not often seen.
They are to be kept at distance, as can be mean.

&****&

Years ago in early morn; I had one in the yard.
I felt lucky to see, and felt he was an Ace card.
He was hungry, and ate birdseed and then left.
We no longer see him and at that I feel bereft.

&*****&

I would not have gone outside to disturb him.
It was not quite light yet, and still quite dim.
They shouldn't be approached as carry rabies.
They are very protective if with their babies.

&*****&

Their face is one of its most distinct features.
They have mask on, and are pretty creatures.
In order to climb well; they have sharp claws.
They are wild and free with environment laws.

&****&

It is illegal to own a wild animal in most states.
If you have a picnic; be sure to pick up plates.
They will come around if you forget some out.
They will knock over trash as they are about.

&****&

The Hawk (Tanka)

The hawk flew up high
He was taking a shower
The sprinkler was on
He needed to cool himself
It was a pleasure to watch

&****&

He flew away then
We drove by in my car then
He was so pretty
I really got a close look
He was on passenger side

&****&

Nature at its best
To see refreshing wildlife
He did feel better
The day was already hot
Sprinkler was relief

&****&

The Eagle (Nonet)

An eagle is a majestic bird
Beauty has no comparison
They hunt with the greatest skill
They have very keen sight
Their wing span is huge
They have great speed
They are proud
Flying
Free

&****&

They
Like Fish
Small mammals
Nest high in tree
Same nest used for years
May hunt with another
Have up to two eggs at once
Fines are given if they are shot
All eagles are endangered species

&****&

Doggy Tales Part 1

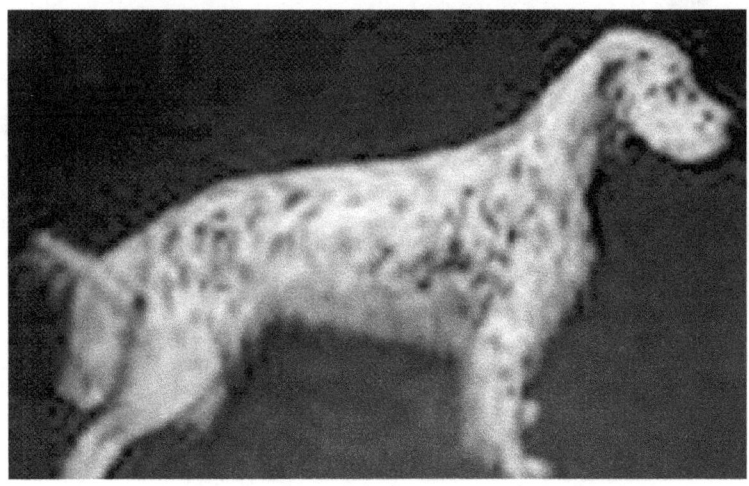

Missy, our English setter began to act strange.
She put her toys under her and did rearrange.
She had been spayed and wanted to be a Mother.
We then got her a friend, unlike any other.

&****&

Missy was happy to have Becky as her friend.
They would play night and day never having an end.
Becky was Gordon setter that she looked after.
Seeing the two together brought us much laughter.

&*****&

I do believe Missy felt like she was her Mom.
She watched her always in case she did something dumb.
We left in the house all day and they would be fine.
Thinking back on this, it was a lovely remind.

&****&

Their kennels were near and they enjoyed the weather.
From inside I could hear them talking together.
When we came home from work, they then came in the house.
They liked to watch the cats play with their small toy mouse.

&****&

Missy enjoyed hunting but Becky never went.
These two dogs we had I believe were heaven sent.
It was fun to watch them play tag in our large yard.
Becky could not outrun, for her this was very hard.

&*****&

These two were just great company for each other.
They were two sisters not in need of a brother.
They got along fine and were both great together.
Their love is imprinted in my heart forever.

&****&

Doggy Tales Part 2

Sherry our Irish setter was learning to hunt.
Among puppy litter we chose her as the runt.
We bought two pigeons and then a couple of quail.
These were to train as she would go on point with tail.

&****&

Hank tucked bird's head under wing putting it to sleep.
Sherry would sniff for the hidden bird which was neat.
She was taught to retrieve and bring back to him.
I went once and we trained until it became dim.

&*****&

Sherry did learn to hunt the birds in this way.
She did look forward to every hunting day.
When birds were not needed, we let them fly away.
There was no point to keep; they did not need to stay.

&*****&

She wore an orange hunting collar with large bell.
As he dressed, she got excited as she could tell.
She would pace in front of the hearth where collar hung.
They would check to be sure they had not stepped in dung.

&****&

Pheasants and small quail are what they hunted the most.
They hunted in many places along the coast.
The meat I marinated for a little while.
We shared with Sherry as she had gone extra mile.

&****&

Doggy Tales Part 3

Sherry our Irish setter was tops in her class.
Hank entered obedience trials as she was fine lass.
She enjoyed the event winning many prizes.
There were competitors with dogs of all sizes.

&****&

She always enjoyed the time spent on these events.
When she did well we always gave treats as presents.
This was quite essential to use throughout her life.
She must obey in the woods or there would be strife.

&****&

On summer day, we traveled an hour for one of these.
She did very well, won a prize, knowing she'd please.
Leaving the arena, Hank then let her run free.
She ran into the lake near us and was carefree.

&****&

She felt so much better now that she was real cool
In a few minutes she was dried off with no drool.
We gave her treats and water before leaving for home.
She was real content now and did not need to roam.

&****&

The First Easter Bunny

A small white bunny wanted to be something great.
He went to Tinniesville and scurried under the gate.
Here all the people were unique in what they did.
As he was small, many hunted him so he hid.

&****&

He heard of a Hot springs in Heathersville quite near.
He knew it did wonders and felt it was sincere.
He did say a prayer that he would be unique.
He bathed in the spring and reflection he did peak.

&****&

He had grown in size to nearly three feet in height!
Now he would find his role that would bring great delight.
He had a dream to deliver treats to the young.
These treats would be all chocolate sweet to the tongue.

&****&

He met with the town elders and told of his plan.
They thought it swell and they did fully understand.
The widow Jane made the best treats and would supply.
They would make this legend and it would never die.

&****&

His whole family would help to deliver too.
All his family went in the spring loving view.
The town paid them by keeping all of them well fed.
They had a fine home and slept in a feather bed.

&****&

This is the story of the first Easter bunny.
At birthday parties they did acts that were funny.
Peter lives in Heathersville now and loves the land.
The predators he had now do think his is grand.

&****&

Peter's First Fundraiser

Tinniesville would be the scene for the first parade.
Plans for a zoo would be used with funds that were made.
Peter rabbit thought of idea in the spring.
Those from Heathersville offered heather and would sing.

&****&

The heather would be used to decorate the floats.
Many would help carrying the heather in totes.
The zoo would be great for neighboring towns as well.
They would advertise in their paper and would tell.

&****&

There would be circus acts and magic shows for all.
People would come by horse and buggy having ball.
The grand finally would be picnic with great food.
All watching parade and acts would be in good mood.

&****&

The town attractions here would be enjoyed by most.
All would speak well of their town and often would boast.
Good will and friendship were felt by all that did care.
The zoo would be a great delight for all to share.

&***&

After all were fed the poets would read a while.
They wrote many things bringing a laugh and a smile.
The preacher would give a sermon and then they left.
All were in joyous mood, no one there was bereft.

&***&

The funds would be used to start a nice zoo in fall.
They needed a plan that would address Peter's call.
The spring parade would be a regular habit.
Elders discussed this plan with Peter the rabbit.

&****&

Peter's Fundraiser Results

Peter's fundraiser efforts were in great demand.
Within both of the towns all there did understand.
Carpenters began to build the shelter for zoo.
All did try to help in whatever they would do.

&****&

On weekends Thumbelina would be there as guest.
Thumbelina was smallest horse if you had guessed.
Having her there at the time was a great pleasure.
Small horse was just seventeen inches by measure.

&*****&

There were bake sales and plays that all did help to raise.
Peter's organizational skills were given praise.
They would have some animals the children could pet.
All here would enjoy zoo, no one would have regret.

&*****&

The sponsors for the zoo would be listed for view.
Visitors here would visit their attractions too.
Heathersville and Tinniesville were towns that brought joy.
Miniature golf was latest and newest toy.

&****&

An artist gallery would have great things for sale.
There was story teller there that read a great tale.
The children enjoyed animal tales that were great.
Some then tried writing and all did appreciate.

&****&

Some animals arrived and were placed at the zoo.
You could buy food to feed and you could pet them too.
The surroundings of zoo were pleasant and pristine.
The caretakers did love all and no one was mean.

&****&

Doggy Tales Part 4

This is about my English setter named Missy.
After reading this, you will know she's not a sissy.
On summer day we put in kennel to get some air.
Hank got home first and took her out getting a scare.

&****&

I guess she had been chasing a bee or wasp.
Her nose was three times its size and it sure did cost!
I immediately called to bring her to the vet.
He prescribed something for allergy, not to fret.

&****&

I can still see this image of her, what a sight!
I am sure this incident gave her a fright.
The medicine in one day brought the swelling down.
She was lively the next day and did play around.

&*****&

I know now they can get allergic reaction.
It's best to check out and get some satisfaction.
Allergies can give different reactions to all.
It is best to get on the phone giving vet a call.

&****&

Doggy Tales Part 5

My dog Missy was diabetic and took shot.
I knew how to give the shot as I had been taught.
My husband Hank would fill for me the required dose,
I would inject her while I was making my toast.

&*****&

She was a good dog and never did shy away.
She received her breakfast after that each day.
We went on mountain vacation to a friend's home.
We brought her meds, food and leash so she would not roam.

&****&

We all had a great week enjoying ourselves much.
She would lie on deck close enough for me to touch.
I would take her for long walks up and down the street.
She enjoyed herself very much and thought it was neat.

&****&

She did not miss Becky, her companion at all.
Our Daughter was caring for Becky and would call.
I felt good that Michelle was not at home alone.
Becky would protect if anyone entered home.

&****&

We enjoyed the mountain air but the week went fast.
The rest we enjoyed but was now a thing in the past.
Becky got excited when she heard the truck arrive.
She rushed to Missy and their friendship did revive.

&*****&

The Zoo Arrivals

Aviary house was built for many types of birds.
Parrots got most visitors because of their words.
The poets had taught them to recite poetry.
All were happy of intelligence they did see.

&****&

There were some chimps that were very gifted as well.
They began to juggle small balls at sound of bell.
There were many bunny species even lop-eared.
All bunnies thought they were special, not at all weird.

&****&

Aquatic plant life was in tanks for all the fish.
Many children would watch all the kinds making wish.
Butterfly house would be available in spring.
Large picnic tables would also be a new thing.

&****&

The bears and tigers would live here most of the year.
They were circus performers that were really dear.
They would be called on when extra funds were needed.
Farmers would be caretakers until crops seeded.

&****&

All animals would be cared for with greatest love.
They would brush and pet them with the softest made glove.
The picnic tables would be placed near babbling brook.
A dozen frogs would harmonize as they all shook.

&****&

They had croaked a special dance called Fred's Froggy stroll.
They happily sung shaking bodies in their knoll.
Later half dozen chickens did their chicken dance.
All enjoyed the acts as some fell into a trance.

&****&

Zoo Job Assignments

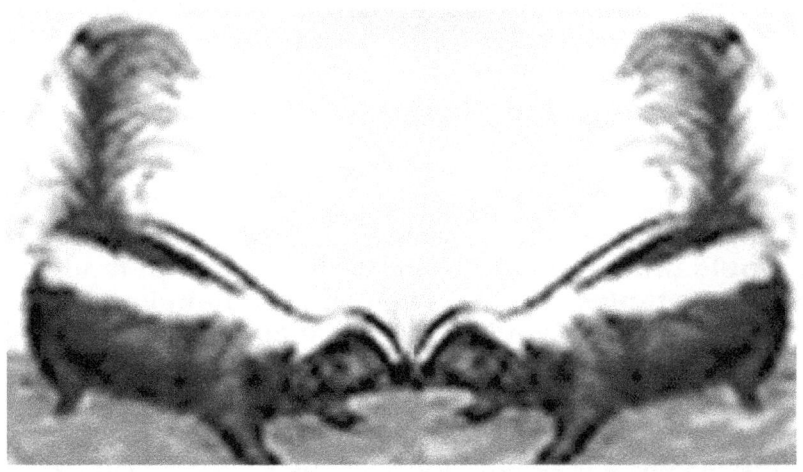

Two skunks approached Peter and asked to be zoo guides.
"We will have to fix your bad scent so no one hides.
I think the Hot springs may be able to help us.
You will ask that you help in zoo and then must trust."

&****&

Flower and Bud went to the springs and took a dip.
They both came out together and shook off each drip.
Flower then said, 'When I spray now I will bring peace."
Bud then said, "When I spray all sadness will then cease."

&****&

"Now we'll bring happiness and peace to all we meet.
All will be happy to see us as we repeat."
"Yes, and we can talk to humans now and that's great!
I know Peter will be glad and appreciate."

&****&

Peter's offspring would sell tickets at the zoo gate.
They counted well as hares multiply at fast rate.
All animals that had gone in spring could talk well.
Peter's new zoo was now the topic in the dell.

&****&

Peter found some residents that would cook on grill.
There were a few cooks that had menus to fulfill.
They would alternate so all had some time at home.
It was not good to leave your wife and kids alone.

&*****&

The zoo gift shop would be run by artist in town.
All that went inside their shop never wore a frown.
The zoo was doing a great business each day.
All did appreciate in their own special way.

&****&

Doggy Tales Part 6

Missy and Becky loved to play outside together.
I would let them run when we had splendid weather.
Their favorite activity was to play with a ball.
Missy outran Becky who usually would fall.

&****&

Together in the house they liked to be with cats.
They all got along, there were never any spats.
The cats would even snuggle up to both of them.
My pets are special and precious as a fine gem.

&****&

They were companions for each other each day.
They appreciated friendship in their own way.
They got lots of exercise outside in our yard.
I did not walk them, two together would be hard.

&*****&

Frisbee was thrown and was Becky's turn to win.
She would jump up so high, and then we would all grin.
Playing with my dogs was always a great pleasure.
Only when they're gone to you begin to measure.

&****&

After we lost Missy, I walked Becky down road.
She liked to go for walks and soon got in the mode.
Right after I fed her supper, I got her leash.
It was exercise for me and peaceful release.

&****&

Heathersville Part 1

Heathersville was a delightful small rural town.
Those that lived here, never ever wore a frown.
The people here were always in a cheerful mood.
All here passed down greatest recipes of food.

&****&

It was lovely country, not like the busy city.
Heather was everywhere and was so pretty.
It was bountiful and town chose it for its name.
The town was tourist attraction and had fame.

&*****&

All wanted to see the house down in the dell.
A lonely widow lived there, but no one could tell.
Her home was built looking like a Gingerbread house.
She did heat with wood, but never had a mouse.

&*****&

She baked gingerbread for all the tourists that came.
Since her home was built; the town was not the same.
The water they drank was from a spring so sweet.
All enjoyed the gingerbread which could not be beat.

&****&

The town was enchanted; all that came never left.
Here all were happy; no one was at all bereft.
Maria's tears always fell in the gingerbread batter.
Loneliness overwhelmed her that was the matter.

&***&

Her loneliness was helped with all that did eat.
It was so good; their visit they would repeat.
Never being a Mom she enjoyed this extended family.
They offered their love and friendship sincerely.

&****&

Heathersville Part 2

Heathersville became the popular place to see.
Hot springs that brought wellness was place to be.
Legend had started with a dream that Maria had.
Husband said in dream; she should not be sad.

&*****&

He told her to believe Hot springs would cure all.
She went into the springs and now stands so tall.
He had seen her suffer from Rheumatoid arthritis before.
She had been crippled, now goes out more and more.

&*****&

She then hitched up her wagon and went into town.
Stepping from buggy all knew wellness she had found.
The Hot springs was down in the valley below.
The sick were then taken there and first to go.

&*****&

The people that believed returned fully well.
Those that did not, shrugged off angrily to tell.
The ride to the spring offered scenery to delight.
Variegated heather fields were everywhere in sight.

&*****&

All the visitors in the town made a point to see her.
They all agreed when they saw, wellness did occur.
They enjoyed the gingerbread she did bake.
Her hands were strong now and did not shake.

&****&

In the valley below homes began to sprout up.
They began to sell their spring water by the cup.
All said after drinking; they felt feeling of peace.
There was no violence in town, all fights did cease.

&****&

Heathersville Part 3

Heathersville now prospers and is on the map.
Lovely couple stayed on teaching how to tap.
Tap dancing is now the latest fun thing, too.
All can do it if you don't have a soft shoe.

&*****&

Maria's yarn was used to make many things.
All are making blankets for the warmth it brings.
Maria's gingerbread is sold at the store.
Most do ask for it when they enter the door.

&****&

Some children see the beauty and start to write.
It's as if they were born poets with insight.
Kids ground heather petals liking what it made.
After adding water; they could paint the glade.

&*****&

Once a month; the town had great dances for all.
Many gifted people looked up to, felt tall.
Poets did read to the crowd and all would love.
All knew their talent came from God up above

&****&

Those that learned how to tap dance would dance so fine.
Later on the dance would stop and they would dine.
There would be great food and gingerbread, divine.
The men would chuckle and go out for some fine wine.

&****&

All in community got along greatly together.
A quill was made from the precious dove feather.
Poets used to write poems that gave the crowd peace.
Children did no mischief, not needing a release.

&*****&

Doggy Tales Part 7

It was a warm spring day so I put Becky out.
In bad weather she did stay in and played about.
She got along well with Missy, our older dog.
Becky was puppy, but ate like a little hog.

&****&

They both did get along well with all of our cats.
Becky played with them, can you imagine that?
The kitties loved to play with their small catnip mouse.
They all did take turns batting it around the house.

&*****&

I always left a few cat toys out for their play.
Becky had a bad tummy ache on a warm spring day.
She moped around house, not wanting to eat at all.
She whimpered, so I thought it best to place a call.

&****&
The vet did an x-ray and gave us the bad news.
She had eaten something, and then I got the blues.
He told us not to worry, of this he was sure.
He gave us some medicine and hoped it would cure.

&*****&
Well the next day, she did not want to go on out.
I put her in her kennel but I did have doubt.
Arriving home from work, I went to bring her in.
The plastic shell of the toy mouse was there within.

&****&
She had eaten the toy, and that is what had gone on.
The cat toys are now put away when we are gone.
We did learn that puppies are very curious.
I was ignorant one, of that I'm furious.

&****&

Doggy Tales Part 8

Grasshoppers were very abundant in this year.
Missy, our English setter enjoyed without fear.
These little critters were everywhere in the yard.
It was easy for her to catch, not at all hard.

&****&

They climbed up tree trunks, trunks became bright solid green.
My dog loved to eat them, which I thought was real mean.
When I took her out for relief, she had a snack.
I would try to stop her, but she launched her attack.

&****&

You could not sit on our porch, because they were there.
It reminded me of locusts and that did scare.
I felt uneasy as I walked in my driveway.
There were great numbers and I sincerely did pray.

&****&

I do not remember year, but it was a sight.
Missy loved them as she found them a great delight.
This was memory I had when I thought of her.
I hope we never get year where this reoccurs.

&*****&

May all your memories of your pets bring you peace.
Writing this verse for you was for me a release.
Treasure your pets while they are with you on this earth
Some of their silly antics can bring you much mirth.

&****&

Heathersville Part 4

Heathersville's elders felt they best do something fast.
They needed an attraction that would really last.
The mayor thought about it and said, "I've a plan.
I'll go see Hope, the good witch, as she'll understand."

&****&

He went to see her and then knew just what to do.
"I will create an Enchanted Forest for you."
Here all species would be friends to one another.
There would be enough food for all kinds of weather.

&*****&

There would be peace and harmony among all here.
All the animals will be gifted and quite dear.
You will receive visitors that want to see this.
All children will visit here and not want to miss.

&*****&

I will cast spell on all creatures and they will stay.
They will raise their families and not want to stray.
"That is great Hope; let us know when we can come see."
"I will send message by my hawk when it will be."

&****&

The spell was great; once they came they never would leave.
She gave peace and love and babies they did conceive.
She gave them magical gifts of verse and dance too.
Some artists created paints form blossoms that grew.

&*****&

She would send a message from her hawk to come view.
Elders would approve this attraction that was new.
They were extremely happy with this creation.
They came back with a glow of anticipation.

&****&

Heathersville Part 5

One day a torn weathered man came to the town.
He looked so sad, and carried a constant frown.
He told the first person he heard of this place.
They offered a ride to see Maria's face.

&*****&

The man looked quite broken, but carried God's book.
They felt Maria better have herself a look.
As soon as she saw him; her heart saw his pain.
"Sir, I need a man to work my farm again.

&****&

I will mend your clothes, and keep you well fed.
The barn has large quarters for a fine bed."
"My name is Joseph Madam, and I do agree.
You will not need to pay me any fee.

&****&

I will be happy to work your farm for you.
My family I lost in a fire; this is true.
I had a wife and two small lassies too.
Please forgive me for babbling on to you?

&****&

May I do something now to show you my worth?"
"Let me feed you first Joseph; then we'll share mirth.
You may wash up in the spring in the glade."
She then began to prepare best meal ever made.

&****&

The Tiger's Plight

The tiger species are in danger of becoming extinct.
They are a master at hunting; this is what I do think.
This large animal needs lots of land in which to roam.
They are better off in the wild than a zoo for a home.

&***&

They are large breed with striped coat in the cat family.
They need to be free in the wild; this I do feel sincerely.
It is a pleasure to see at zoo, but they need to be free.
God created to live in woods; this is how is should be.

&***&

The area for all of our wildlife diminishes each year.
It seems to be quite a problem, causing to shed a tear.
Our lands are now getting exploited, for so many things.
The world is overusing our resources and chaos it brings.

&***&

I pray that our God will correct this error of man today.
We seem to do so much for profit, what more can I say.
Support wildlife endangered species whenever you can.
This does benefit all, and shows we are making a stand.

&****&

The Flying Squirrel

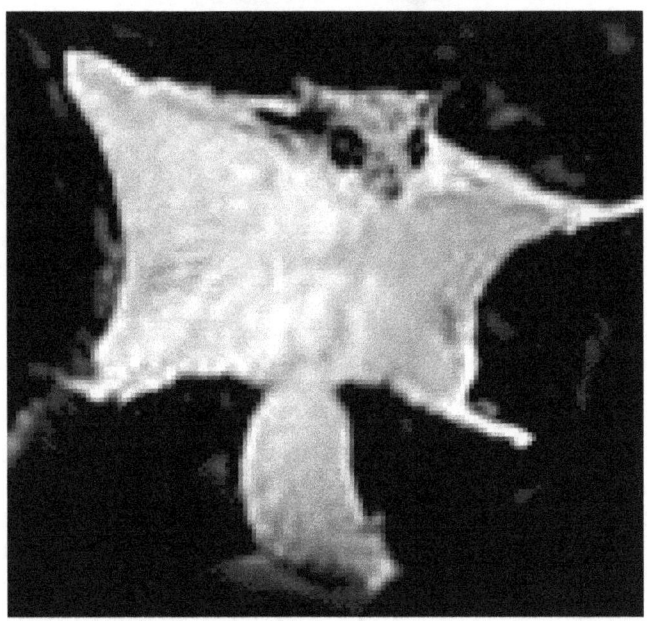

The flying squirrel is a cute creature to see.
They are nocturnal, may be seen gliding on a tree.
They do not actually have wings, but they resemble a bat.
They would be a delightful dinner for a kitty cat.

&****&

A friend down the street has three that she feeds.
They enjoy all the great sunflower seeds.
She watches from inside the house shining a light.
They are not scared and do not run away in fright.

&****&

They are a little smaller in size than the average grey.
If I ever saw one, that would surely make my day.
I believe they are faster than the kind I see.
You can watch a video on the internet for free.

&****&

Heathersville Part 6

Joe was hard worker and Maria was impressed.
She felt better knowing his background he confessed.
They began to work together on her farm.
She fell in love with him; he was like a charm.

&****&

The first town dance they attended together.
Maria wanted him to be with her forever.
She saw something she had never seen before.
He was greatest comic ever came in that door.

&****&

They all loved the comical scenes he would tell.
Maria knew for sure now her heart did swell.
She then interrupted and asked him for a dance.
"Joe; I been meaning to tell you our love has a chance.

&****&

Will you love as my husband, and give all your love?"
"I do love you and have been sent from God above.
My love; let me, Joseph, announce our wedding date."
Maria smiled and he then announced their fate.

&****&

The entire town clapped as they saw their love.
They danced together expertly like a hand and glove.
Preparations would begin now for their marriage.
Maria prays someday she will push a baby carriage.

&****&

Heathersville Part 7

The wedding would be in spring when all came alive.
The heather plants had multiplied and did thrive.
Maria would make herself the prettiest dress.
She wanted to be lovely; this she did confess.

&****&

One day, Joe worked very hard shearing the sheep's wool.
Afterwards he wanted to fish when it got cool.
He asked her if she wanted to go to the lake.
She chuckled saying, she would stay home to bake.

&****&

She needed to work on her dress for their wedding.
She made sure when he returned, no wool was shedding.
He was able to catch catfish for their dinner.
He picked heather knowing he would be a winner.

&****&

Catfish and the flowers surely would make her smile.
Catfish dinner with gingerbread was worth the mile.
He had walked to lake to get some exercise.
It always felt good and he felt it was wise.

&****&

He told Maria the species was called catfish.
He found a tiny black kitten, making a wish.
He then picked up the kitten and gave him to her.
Her eyes welled with tears of joy and then did blur.

&****&

"Oh Joe, this kitty is such a darling; I love him."
Maria knew she would be happy, things never dim.
Together they made a soft bed for the kitten.
Their love was shown on their face, love quite smitten.

&****&

The Bear Family

There were Brad, Betty and Beverly; that made three.
They said their prayers every night on bended knee.
They lived in the large cave on the hill.
They were kind and no one did want to kill.

&*****&

Betty made oatmeal each day before they went for a walk.
They would wander a little and pleasantly talk.
They returned on this day to find no oatmeal in dish.
Brad said, "I hope whoever ate this is full; that is my wish."

&*****&

"We can always make some more to eat.
Some people do not eat regularly; it is a treat.
Let us thank God for all our blessings.
Does anyone now have any confessing?"

&****&

"It maybe was the new squirrel family down the road a bit.
Betty will you kindly made some more before Bev has a fit?
You must remember to share with those that have less.
Betty dear; I will help you will all of this mess."

&*****&

The Prairie Dog (Haiku/Senyru)

**Prairie dog give thanks
He has seen his shadow
Spring is nearly here**

&**&**

**Lifespan is quite short
Live between three to five years
Endangered species**

&**&**

They live underground
They have many predators
They have no defense

&****&

They can only hide
They fear hawks, owls and eagles
Coyotes also

&****&

Weigh two to three pounds
Target practice for hunters
Resemble a squirrel

&****&

They are killed with ease
They stand perfectly still
They need to be saved

&****&

Funds needed to save
Give to fund for protection
They are quite unique

&***&

The Sly Skunk (Haiku/Quatrain)

A girl skunk was born
She was given name Flower
Her spray was so sweet

&****&

She was so unique
She had no defense at all
She had to use care

&****&

She would be quite wise
Would act with great bravery
From distance all fled

&***&

A fine male found her
They mated and had babies
She was skunk's "supreme"

&****&

She was unique for a reason
Her talents she used in pleasing
She never did follow the crowd
She never did have to be loud

&****&

Like humans she used gift quite well
Handicap she never did tell
All did look up to her for this
She kept her mate in complete bliss

&****&

The Miniature Donkeys

The miniature donkeys were their latest pets.
They got in golden years without any regrets.
Their first donkey was called Buttercup and was grey.
They mated at farm down the road on a spring day.

&****&

Their Buttercup later bore a babe called Jenny.
Their Grandkids loved her like the shiniest penny.
She was also a greyest color like her Mom.
These donkeys are quite affectionate not dumb.

&****&

The family got a female to be her friend.
Buttercup and Sarah would be the newest trend.
Sarah was her name and she was darker black.
They both had the legendary star on their back.

&****&

Later Sarah was taken to farm for a mate.
The following year babe would be born as was fate.
They can live between thirty to thirty-five years.
These precious animals do not have any fears.

&****&

At Two Hundred Fifty pounds they are really small.
At Four Hundred Fifty pounds they are among tall.
They are very affectionate and show their love.
The star on their back shows there loved by God above.

&****&

Glossary of Poetry Forms 1

Lucky Leaf--- a poetry form created by Christina R Jussaume on 08 22 07. The form should be center aligned to give shape of clover. Syllables are 3, 3, 9, 9, 12, 12, 6, 6, 3, and 3. It can be any subject with or without rhyme.

Michelle's Heart---a poetry form created by Christina R Jussaume on 08 10 07. I created this shaped poetry form for my Daughter Michelle. It is a poem of 11 lines. Syllable count is 3,3,5,8,9,10, 8, 7, 5, 3, and 3.
 Subject is optional. It should be center aligned and it looks like a heart.
Rhyme scheme is ABBCCDDEFGH

Joseph & Christina... a poetry form created by Christina R Jussaume on 08 07 07 in memory of her parents. It begins with a Joseph's Star, a poem without rhyme in 1, 3, 5, 7, 7, 5, 3 and 1. These lines should have full statements. Then it begins the next part written for Mom (Christina also) which resembles a cross. This poem is 5 stanzas of 3 rhyming lines each. Stanza one... 5syllables, Stanza two...10 syllables, stanza 3 - 5 all have 5 syllables. The entire poem must be centered aligned to give you the appearance of a star and a cross. Subject can be love, spiritual, or nature.

Joseph's Star... a poetry from created by Christina R Jussaume on 08 06 07 in memory of my Dad. This poem has no rhyme. It is just written according to syllable
counts. Syllables are 1, 3, 5, 7, 7, 5, 3, and 1. It should have complete statements in each line. It can be about any subject. It should be center aligned. There is no limit to the number of stanzas you create. It can be about any subject.

Glossary of Poetry Forms 2

Fable
A fable is a poetic story composed in verse or prose with a moral summed up at the end. Usually animals are used as characters to teach a valuable lesson.

Nonet
A Nonet has nine lines. The first line has nine syllables, the second line eight syllables, the third line seven syllables, etc... until line nine that finishes with one syllable. It can be on any subject and rhyming is optional. Then a reverse Nonet starts with 1 syllable continuing until you reach 9 syllables.

Line 1 - 9 syllables
Line 2 - 8 syllables
Line 3 - 7 syllables
Line 4 - 6 syllables
Line 5 - 5 syllables
Line 6 - 4 syllables
Line 7 - 3 syllables
Line 8 - 2 syllables
Line 9 - 1 syllable

Quatrain
A Quatrain is a poem consisting of four lines of verse with a specific rhyming scheme.

A <u>few</u> examples of a quatrain rhyming scheme are as follows:

#1) abab
#2) abba -- envelope rhyme
#3) aabb
#4) aaba, bbcb, ccdc, dddd -- chain rhyme

Glossary of Poetry Forms 3

Tanka
Tanka is a classic form of Japanese poetry related to the haiku with five unrhymed lines of five, seven, five, seven, and seven syllables. (5, 7, 5, 7, 7)
The 5/7/5/7/7 rule is rumored to have been made up for school children to understand and learn this type of poetry. For an in depth description of Haiku, please visit the Shadow Poetry Haiku, Senryu, and Tanka section.

Canzone
An Italian lyric poem usually 4 or 5 stanzas followed by a short envoi summarizing the poem. Syllable count for this is 11, 7, 11, 7, for each stanza, followed by a two line envoi summarizing the poem.

Haiku
Most popular definition, but there is more to haiku than meets the eye:

Haiku (also called nature or seasonal haiku) is an unrhymed Japanese verse consisting of three unrhymed lines of (5,7,5) or 17 syllables in all. Haiku is usually written in the present tense and focuses on nature (seasons).

The 5/7/5 rule was made up for school children to understand and learn this type of poetry. for an in depth description of Haiku, please visit the Shadow Poetry
Haiku, Senryu, and Tanka

Senryu
Most popular definition, but there is more to senryu than meets the eye:

Glossary of Poetry Forms 4

Senryu (also called human haiku) is an unrhymed Japanese verse consisting of three unrhymed lines of five, seven, and five syllables (5, 7, 5) or 17 syllables in all. Senryu is usually written in the present tense and only references to some aspect of human nature or emotions. They possess no references to the natural world and thus stand out from nature/seasonal haiku.

The 5/7/5 rule was made up for school children to understand and learn this type of poetry.
For an in depth description of Haiku, please visit the Shadow Poetry
Haiku, Senryu and Tanka section.
There is much more to senryu than the made up 5/7/5 version.

Free Verse
Free Verse is an irregular form of poetry in which the content free of traditional rules of versification,
(freedom from fixed meter or rhyme).

In moving from line to line, the poet's main consideration is where to insert line breaks. Some ways
of doing this include breaking the line where there is a natural pause or at a point of suspense for the
reader.

Patricia's Harmony
This form was created by Christina R Jussaume as a tribute to poet
Patricia Ann Farnsworth Simpson. The form starts with 4 senryu. These senyru begin with the letters P A T R I C I A S H A R. Next 8 syllable count quatrain in rhyme. This must start with letters M O N Y.
The poem must be spiritual in nature.. I have incorporated an acrostic, senyru and quatrain style within this style of mine.

"My Walk With Jesus"

My First book by PublishAmerica.
This collection is a Poetry book of God and Nature.
It is available at Amazon and Barnes and Noble.
Read more about this and all my poetry at my own website
www.PoetessCRJussaume.com

I lost both of my parents before I was forty years of age.
By writing poetry I found relief from the grief.
My poetry helped me to see the beauty given by God.
The beauty I had seen all of my life I began to write about. This collection of poems expresses my faith.
With God in my life I handled all things put before me.
This collection is written with the essence of my heart and soul.
These words I express with a sincere heart.
Now won't you take this walk with me to see the beauty
God has given all around us? Enjoy the beauty of
rose gardens and magnificent sunsets
as I bring them all to life within my poems.
I felt peace as I wrote this collection and now
this peace I so happily share with you.

Christina R Jussaume

www.pfppublishers.com

www.ingramcontent.com/pod-product-compliance
Lightning Source LLC
Chambersburg PA
CBHW022132080426
42734CB00006B/336